The House of Tiny Tearaways

Dr Tanya Byron is a clinical psychologist who has worked within the UK's National Health Service for sixteen years. She has in-depth experience of working and teaching in many aspects of mental health and psychology. She specializes in treating children, teenagers and families with psychological, emotional and behavioural difficulties in a wide range of areas. She has two young children of her own.

Tanya is the co-author of *Little Angels* (BBC Books) and has filmed several series for screening on the BBC including *Little Angels, Teen Angels* and *The House of Tiny Tearaways*.

Published by BBC Active, an imprint of Educational Publishers LLP, part of the Pearson Education Group. Edinburgh Gate, Harlow, Essex, CM20 2JE

First published 2005
Third impression 2015

This book is published to accompany the television series, *The House of Tiny Tearaways*, first broadcast on BBC THREE and BBC TWO in 2005.

Executive producers: Laura Mansfield, Martin Scott
Commissioning Executive: Suzanne Gilfillan

The House of Tiny Tearaways is an Outline Productions and BBC Format Entertainment co-production for BBC THREE. Licensed by RDF Rights.

ISBN: 978-0-563-52036-8

Commissioning Editor: Emma Shackleton
Project Editor: Sarah Sutton
Assistant Project Editor: Jeanette Payne
Copy Editor: Helena Caldon
Designer: Annette Peppis
Photographer: Chris Capstick
Picture Researcher: Emma Young
Production Controller: Man Fai Lau

Set in Optima and Cosmos
Printed and bound in China (CTPS/03).

For more information about this and other BBC books, please call 08700 777 001 or visit our website on www.bbcshop.co.uk

The House of Tiny Tearaways

Dr Tanya Byron

Contents

In memory of my dear father,
John Sichel,
who died during the filming of the first series.

And for my mother Elfie, and my sister Katrina,
with all my love.

Inside *The House of Tiny Tearaways*

The House

The House of Tiny Tearaways is a television series created to put child behaviour and parenting problems under the professional spotlight in a safe and constructive way. The House itself was designed to be a sanctuary for families who were at the end of their tether. The design and construction of the House was completed in conjunction with a committee of childcare experts, who made sure that it was a safe, fun place for kids to stay, whilst also recreating a realistic and practical home environment. The remote cameras – and those located behind two-way mirrors – allow me to observe the pitfalls and progress, the tantrums and the tears of the families, 24-hours-a-day, without intruding on their lives.

Any television programme that involves the observation of real people in real time runs the risk of playing to the audience and exploiting the emotions of those who take part. It is very important to all of us involved in *The House of Tiny Tearaways* that the personal lives of those involved will not be used gratuitously. As a clinical psychologist, I work in a profession which operates within distinct guidelines and keeps to a clearly-defined code of conduct. Observations are made and advice is given founded on evidence-based considerations. All the time I am working in the House I am conscious of these professional ethical considerations and, with the support of the production team, work hard to make sure that the emotional needs of the families remain the central priority. My principle job is to work with the families.

'This series gave me a unique opportunity as a practitioner to experience what happens to families once they leave the consulting room, and then continue working with them.'

The families

Throughout the series the privacy of the families is safeguarded. Personal boundaries are discussed, agreed and maintained at all times. Not everything that is discussed is revealed on the television screens, and professional integrity is retained at all times. These safeguards are critical for the experience to be a positive and constructive one for individuals who are in an intense and vulnerable state. Many of the families chosen to be part of this unique programme are at the point of 'make or break' in their relationship with their children and with their partners.

Working in such an exposed and intense environment is a major challenge for them, as well as for me. I need to be able to talk to them robustly to be able to help – and they need to feel safe in revealing personal experiences to me.

The consultation experience

It is an immense challenge to take on the task of clearly understanding and responding to the problems presented by each of our *Tearaway* families in a six-day period. I am acutely aware that the artificial and intense environment within the house would be in complete contrast to the 'normal' lives of the families, and it is important not to create a short-lived 'quick fix' for the sake of the television cameras. For this reason, each day of the experience is carefully planned:

- Day one is a 'settling in and getting to know' day for the families which allows me time to observe them together and acting in their normal way.
- Day two focuses on me getting to know each member of the family and introducing behavioural techniques to parents to help them overcome extreme behaviours.
- Day three generally continues with the parent training and, through consultation, parents often start to reveal what I call 'the back story': the personal history or difficult experience that is driving the parental responses to their child.
- Day four sees a continuation of activities and tasks to support the behavioural work that is being done and to help parents to come to terms with their personal history, thereby detaching its power from their relationship with their child.
- Day five is about brushing up on the techniques that have been learned and gradually becoming disengaged from the House. For some parents there are outings away from the House to help them to develop their skills in a generalized environment. For others there are spoken and written commitments to help them to mark and acknowledge the milestones reached in their relationships.
- Day six is about leaving the House – and how to maintain learned behaviours once they have left. The biggest challenge is in helping families to develop the self-belief that when they leave the security of the House they will be able to maintain the new behaviours in their home environments.

We follow up with each of the families two weeks later, and beyond. Just because we finish filming does not mean that the problems go away. All of the families have access to help if they need it. Several of them have remained in contact.

The great news is that all of the families are doing well (see Chapter 8) – these techniques, combined with behavioural awareness, bring about real change.

The advisory panel

From the outset the production team consulted with a panel of four leading experts in the field of child welfare to ensure that at every stage the children's health and safety, both physical and mental, were at the very centre of their planning.

The panel commended the team's 'highly professional' approach to the project and congratulated them on their attentiveness to the welfare of the children.

Note to readers

Throughout this book the word 'parents' has been used to represent birth parents, step-parents, adoptive parents, foster parents, partners and any carer who is the main role model and influence in a child's life.

In the main I have referred to 'your child' throughout, rather than children, step-children, adopted or foster children, because every adult's relationship with every child is unique and special. The issues and techniques discussed in the book remain relevant whether or not you gave birth to your child and however many children there are in your family.

In our modern society there are many different family models and many different cultural influences. Although I take into account the particular challenges of sole-parenting, the shape, size, origin or special needs of your family will be of less importance in your child's development than the consistent and caring way you act as positive role models, and the love and enthusiasm you have for your child.

'I loved the thought of all the families living together, giving each other help and support.'

Introduction

Those of you who have watched *The House of Tiny Tearaways* will know the powerful life-changing effect that the experience of living in the House has on the lives of the families who participated.

Sets of three families stay in the House for six days at a time. During that time, the House becomes much more than a home: it was a safe environment and a supportive community, where the families could work with me to discover the real problems that were underlying their children's difficult behaviour. Our work together achieved remarkable results – and revealed interesting answers to some very desperate parents' prayers.

The first series in particular was a very personal experience for me because the families – and I – were going into unchartered clinical territory. The surprise for me as a clinical psychologist was the speed of the results brought about in an intense group environment. It reinforced my awareness of the value of community and the importance of having personal support when trying to overcome children's and families' behavioural problems.

This aspect of my work is central to this book. When we are under pressure there is a natural tendency to retreat from the world and to hide or suppress problems – but I will be recommending ways to face and embrace your problems 'full on' and to gather around you a support network of trusted friends and family. Viewers identified with the families who were struggling to cope with their tearaway toddlers. In real life not everyone has the space and time to spend with a clinical psychologist, and there is only one 'House of Tiny Tearaways'.

Parents whose children have developed severe behavioural problems feel isolated: they feel alone with their problem, many develop low self-esteem as parents, and are often unwilling to admit to – or share – their difficulties with others. But there is no need to be ashamed of wilful behaviour in your child. It is often a healthy sign, and a natural part of child development.

The reality is that all parents struggle with the issues of how and when to discipline a child, feel guilty that they do not spend enough time playing with their children, fear being judged harshly for being unable to control bad behaviour, suffer from lack of sleep, and fall out with their partner over what to do 'for the best'. These are normal challenges and do not make you a bad parent. I often feel more concerned when I meet a compliant child whose spirit has been repressed than when I meet a child who is rebelling against the rules and boundaries of life.

We all make mistakes. Being a good parent is not about being perfect; adults, like children, have to be allowed to make mistakes in order to learn. The important thing is to recognize when things have gone wrong, to 'own up' and to take responsibility for your role in the problem.

In writing this book I wanted to share the parenting techniques and insights that I have learned during my years as a clinical psychologist – so that you and your child learn to manage disruptive behaviours, and so that you can bond with your child and learn how to enjoy being a parent again.

People often say to me, 'You're a clinical psychologist, so your children must be perfect. You must be the best mother in the world.' What I say is: being a clinical psychologist doesn't make me a better mother – but being a mother makes me a better practitioner, because I can empathize with the feelings of the parents.

The value of community

The environment within the House of Tiny Tearaways encourages each group of three families to become a supportive community quite quickly during their stay – and this in turn accelerates the learning process. The same effect occurs in 'real' life amongst close communities or groups of friends.

It is useful to take stock and to be aware of who is in your personal community – to remind you that you are not alone.

- Who would you normally turn to in a crisis? They are a crucial part of your community.
- Think of others in a similar situation to yourself who you respect.
- Consider who amongst your friends and families you can trust.
- Remember that you have professionals as well as friends in your community: your doctor, health visitor, teachers, psychologist.

'Being a clinical psychologist doesn't make me a better mother – but being a mother makes me a better practitioner.'

Having a sense of community comes through building and using social networks. It also develops from having the courage to be honest and by taking the risk of trusting others enough to share your experiences with them.

The value of honesty

The key to the success of the community in the House is honesty. Everyone is very honest about their problems, their history, and what they are going through. As a result it becomes easier for others to open up and talk about their issues.

There are other people close to you geographically, who have encountered the problem you are currently facing. Understanding that others are experiencing the same thing as you has the effect of normalizing the problem, and turns it into something that can be understood, managed and overcome. If you understand that 'I am not a bad parent, and we are all struggling', your awareness will destigmatize the problem and broaden your focus, away from your child.

Having a sense of community and developing an awareness of others broadens personal horizons. Problems can be isolating, and parents can become obsessive and over-focused on the child who is causing them

'This place is cool.'

Harrison Dixon

concern. Sharing knowledge with others is an empowering way of learning from experience.

Your experience will help others, too. If you can help others to overcome their problem successfully, then you will realize that you can't be all bad as a parent. If you can also learn from the experience of others, then you will feel less isolated and more secure in the belief that things can change.

Children will benefit from communities too

Like adults, children learn through personal experience and from the experience of others. Children learn through play; they learn from their parents and carers, they learn from those they meet in everyday life, and they learn from each other.

The safe, fun environment of the House had a powerful impact on the social learning skills of children for several reasons:

- They sensed that their parents were happier and more relaxed.
- They responded immediately to the play-orientated environment.
- Their developmental progress sped up as a result of exposure to the other children – especially at mealtimes.

The same environment and benefits can be created at home, in the car, at a friend's house – anywhere. The important element is to make sure that positive parenting and creative play are at the heart of everything you do.

In the main a child's behaviour has its roots in his or her relationship with their parent – and the parents' relationship with each other (even if one parent is absent).

The next two chapters look at issues that form the foundation stones of positive parenting: your parenting skills and the power of creative play. The remainder of the book looks at behavioural issues, including sleep and eating problems, offering positive, nurturing and practical strategies to help manage and overcome them.

1 Transform Your Parenting Skills

Children are highly intuitive and understand much more about what is going on in a household than might be apparent from their language skills or physical development. Often this impacts on their behaviour. A child who is constantly disruptive may be unhappy, and a child who is always acting in an angry fashion may be acutely anxious or sad and hurt inside.

Children's behaviour is frequently an indicator of parental mood or the state of the parents' relationship. This chapter looks at parenting styles and how life is experienced from the child's perspective, including:

- What motivates your child's behaviour.
- What you want for your family.
- How your personal 'story' may subconsciously affect your parenting style.
- How every parent can enhance their positive parenting skills.

What motivates your child's behaviour?

Children, like adults, have a great need to feel loved and have a sense of belonging. But whereas an adult is aware that we are all individuals and separate from each other, a young child is egocentric – believing that he is the centre of your world, and you are the centre of his. He or she gets his or her early sense of self-worth from the level and kind of attention that they receive from you, the parent/s.

As a result, small children are attention-seekers. They love getting your interest as it reinforces their sense of security and identity. They learn from an early age what kinds of behaviour capture your attention – and whatever it is, you will get more of it! In simple terms: if you pay more attention to your child when they are 'good' than when they are 'bad', you will get more good behaviour than bad behaviour. But, if you are short on praise and long on telling off, your child may well respond by increasing their naughty behaviour – because being naughty is what gets him or her noticed.

This behavioural pattern becomes more complicated where there is discord or unhappiness in the family. Children often believe themselves to be the cause of problems in the home and that they are natural 'fixers'. The 'fixing' does not always come across in a constructive fashion, but it will succeed in getting your attention – which is the desired result.

There were several couples in the House of Tiny Tearaways who acknowledged that they would probably have drifted apart had

Dr Tanya says...

'The main question is not how to solve the problem, but how we can get to the bottom of why the problems are there in the first place.'

concern about their child's behaviour not kept them communicating. A child who is distressed by parental rows and antagonism soon learns that if they 'draw fire' mummy and daddy will start talking again. It's their bad behaviour that unites the parents.

Not every child has major problems. A situation does not need to be extreme for you to feel that your child has behavioural issues that you would like some help with. Sometimes the behavioural 'blip' can be the simple result of parents trying to juggle too many responsibilities in a busy lifestyle, and not planning how and when to spend enough time with their child.

Chapter 5 looks at behavioural problems and how to manage them, in practical detail. This chapter looks at the behavioural triggers within families that cause the problems in the first place.

Getting to the root of the problem

My role as a clinical psychologist working with families is threefold:

- To get to the root cause of each child's behavioural problems.
- To understand whether the child's behaviour is a manifestation of bigger underlying problems in their environment, such as school, home, etc.
- To help families to turn destructive behaviour patterns into positive ones.

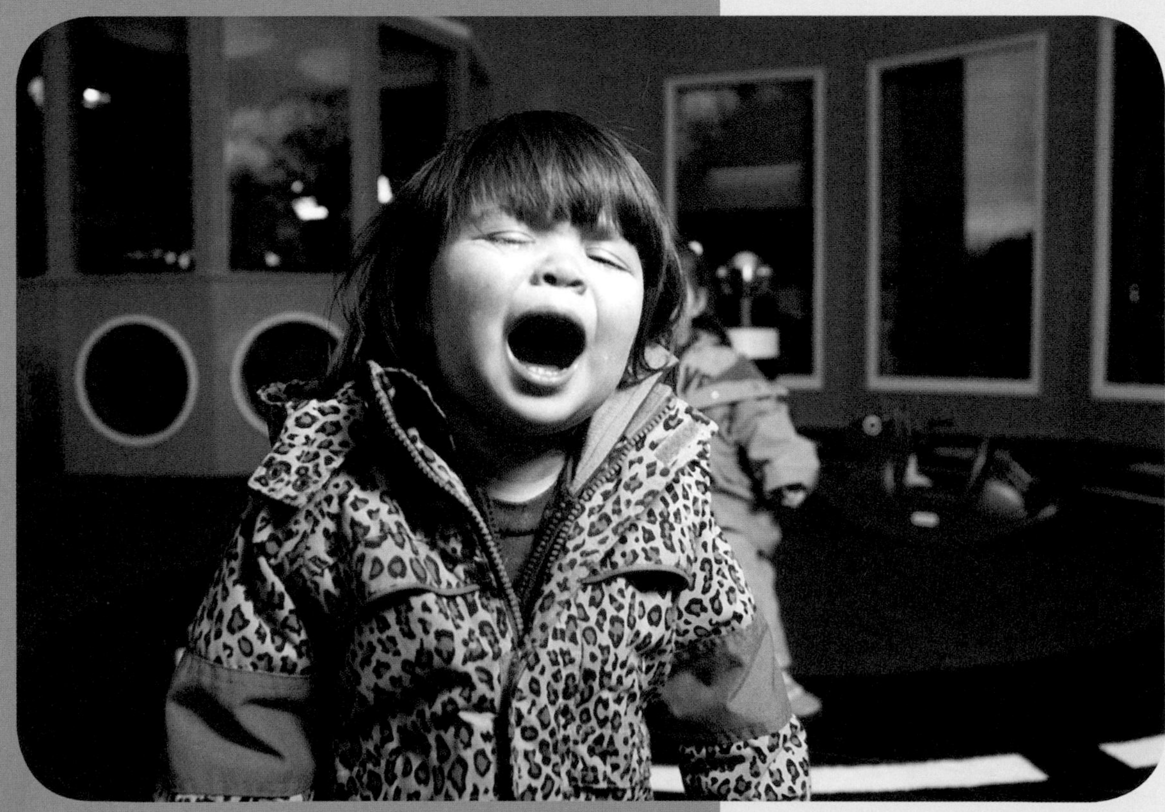

'Your childhood experiences will affect your parenting style.'

In many ways giving parents behavioural tools to help shape their kids' behaviour is the easy bit. Getting to the heart of the underlying behaviour is more of a challenge; and if behaviours are entrenched and the problems are serious, bringing about lasting change can take months.

It amazed me that in the safe environment of the House – away from life's distractions and with nothing else to focus on – how quickly the 'story' of each family was revealed, and how quick and ready each couple was to embrace positive change. It is a tribute to those parents that they managed to keep those changes going when they returned home. (See Chapter 8: A Life-Changing Formula.)

What is a 'good' parent?

Parenting is a job for life which comes without a rulebook. Our own childhood experiences tend to be our starting point for learning what works and what doesn't. We emulate the past if our experience was positive and we avoid past mistakes if it was negative. Invariably, as children begin to grow up, there will be times when we feel we have 'failed' as parents; that we're 'not good enough' or are 'undeserving'.

If you were to ask any adult what they valued most in their parents as children, and what they would like to bring to their own parenting, the following qualities are likely to be fairly high up on their list:

- Love and affection.
- Trust and feeling safe.
- Knowing what to expect.
- Fun and playfulness.
- Clear rules and boundaries.
- Doing things together.
- Encouragement and praise.
- Acceptance of 'who I am'.
- A sense of joy.
- A sense of 'family'.

These traits are unrelated to money, status or where you live; they do not depend upon the size, shape, or ethnic origin of your family. They are qualities that are linked to love, nurture and a sense of belonging in life.

Good parenting comes from the heart. It is consistent, loving, tough but fair, and sets a good example. Good parenting involves accepting the uniqueness of your child, and helping children to develop the confidence to enjoy being themselves.

The importance of personal commitment

As every parent knows, it takes more than reading a book or watching a television series to transform a child's behaviour. The common features amongst parents who succeed in turning a child's problems around is their:

- Utter commitment to their children.
- Courage in recognizing personal issues that were affecting their parenting.
- Determination to take a unified approach to parenting.
- Willingness to stick to the programme.
- Self-belief.
- Belief in the methods and the knowledge that they work.

Those who watched *The House of Tiny Tearaways* will know that the parents' commitment to keep going, even when it was painful to do so, was both humbling and powerful to watch.

Behaviour-shaping

Parents have a responsibility to help their children shape their behaviour so that they understand the difference between 'right' and 'wrong'. They also need to encourage them to develop the social, communication and reasoning skills to survive, and to have the self-discipline and motivation to thrive in adult life.

Behaviour-shaping isn't necessarily about encouraging your child to be constantly well-behaved or 'good'; it is about self-expression and understanding what is appropriate behaviour in different circumstances. Behaviour-shaping enables your children to learn and gives them the tools and skills they need.

If your child does something well, show them that they are doing it well and positively reinforce that behaviour. Positive reinforcement helps children to

'A child who plays up at home, but not at school, needs clearer boundaries.'

move forward with confidence. If they make a mistake, get them to understand it was a mistake and to learn that you don't want them to do that again. The contrast between these two approaches will help your child to understand how you want them to behave.

Your child is learning all through his or her life – and that learning is a process. The process meanders like a river: it's not a linear approach. Parents will say, 'they were doing so well and then they took a backward step', but it's not a backward step, they just moved into another developmental stage. Every time your child has another set of experiences they will meander in their learning. Behaviour shaping is about being calm and flexible enough to keep your child confident and on track.

Dr Tanya says...
'Help children to understand the experiences that they are having and find ways of helping your child to express or verbalize what is going on.'

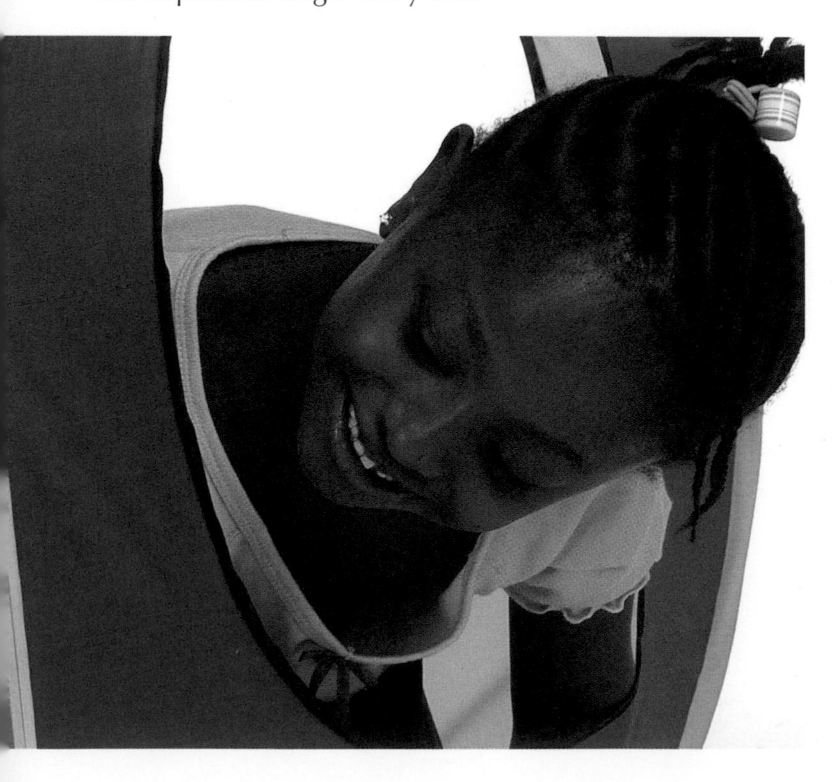

Behaviour needs to be considered in the context of the child's character. There are occasions when being rebellious, cheeky or irreverent is equally appropriate behaviour, and has the benefit of being entertaining and lifting a mood.

Children change and develop at different rates. Be aware of the individual: don't be tempted to compare your child with your friend's children and if you have several children, resist comparing one with another. They each have skills, they each have needs, they each have different strengths.

The key is to understand the long-term consequences of your parenting style. With every parenting decision you make today, you are sowing the seeds of the teenager of tomorrow.

What sort of family life do you want?

Take a while to consider:

- What kind of family life do you want?
- Does it differ from the one you have at the moment?
- Does it share characteristics with your own childhood, or are you motivated by a desire not to repeat the past?
- What are your overall memories of family life? Are they positive or negative?
- What sort of relationship did you have, or have you got, with your parents?
- Can you see characteristics of their parenting style in your own approach? How do you feel about that?

There are no right or wrong answers to these questions, but taking time to consider your answers will give you the space to take stock and envisage what it is you want for yourself as a parent and for your own children.

Take stock of your relationships

Although this book is not primarily about adult relationships, it is concerned with the parental relationship – how your ability to express love and intimacy, or hostility and anger impacts on your relationship with your child and affects his or her development.

The following questions will help you to think about your role and relationship:

- How would you describe each of your children?
- How would you describe your relationship with each of your children?
- How would you describe yourself as a parent?
- How would you describe your partner?
- How would you describe your relationship with your partner (or the absent parent if you are a sole parent)?
- How would you describe yourself as a partner?
- What do you want from each other?
- What are your priorities for change?
- What do you think are the obstacles to change?

A loving relationship between two adults is highly personal and goes through many changes as each individual grows and adapts. Sometimes people grow apart or find they are travelling on parallel lines and have forgotten how to communicate.

If you are content with your current relationship and secure knowing that you are loved and can express your affection to your partner and to your children it will be easier for you to bring about positive change.

If you feel you are in a fractured partnership, now could be the time to take stock. Don't be afraid to seek professional help if you feel you need some objective assistance in understanding and addressing your relationship issues.

No matter how much we may dream of the fairytale ending, no family is perfect and nor should it be: there is little room for learning, growth and variety in a perfect environment. However, some people have experienced more tragedy than others; and not every parent had the best of role models in their own upbringing. Although it may be painful, it is vital to be able to look your past in the face and to understand and come to terms with its impact on your present if you are to be free of its negative influence.

Dr Tanya says...

'Don't live your life through your child, and don't try to repair the disasters in your own life by projecting them onto your child.'

Facing up to the past

Take some quiet time to consider whether there been any traumatic events in your life that may have:

- affected your ability to express your emotions honestly and openly.
- increased your sensitivity to the possibility of separation or rejection.
- damaged your perception of yourself as lovable.
- damaged your perception of yourself as a worthy parent.

Time may be a great healer in terms of enabling us to cope with past loss and trauma, but if all you have done is deny your pain and repress its consequences, the negative impact on your sense of self-worth will be significant. Your emotional responses to past events will escape no matter how carefully you try to contain them or protect yourself from them; causing unwanted distress and anxiety when you are at your most vulnerable. Children are often the easiest target for the projection of excess adult baggage.

As all the parents in the House found, almost without exception, understanding the events and experiences that have shaped our own development and responses, enables us to replace negative beliefs and anxieties with positive beliefs and reinforcement. Like children, most adults want to experience love, affection and trust in their home environment and to feel safe to express themselves without being judged. That can only happen in an atmosphere of honesty and forgiveness.

Managing secrecy

Quite often at the heart of a child's behaviour problem is a family secret of some sort that is hidden 'for the good of the child'. This may relate to a miscarriage, an affair, a previous marriage, an adoption, an illness, a fraud, or other variations on the theme. Deciding whether to disclose a secret to a child is a personal decision that depends upon the circumstances and on the maturity of the child. A child does not necessarily need to know about adult secrets until they are old enough to understand and are able to process the information.

The important thing is not so much the facts, but that the parents themselves are open and honest with each other about their response to the secret, how it might be impacting on their relationship with each other and with their child. The priority for the parent is to find a way to separate any inner emotional conflict from their feelings towards their child. If there is 'unfinished business' a child will pick up on the vibe over time, even if the issue itself is not discussed directly. They are very likely to concoct their own alternative version of reality if there is no explanation.

Longer term, there is a balance to be found between choosing not to disclose something important, and withholding it for so long that the secret itself, rather than the facts of the matter, eventually becomes a betrayal of trust.

Shifting beliefs

Every family has a unique story: past events and childhood experiences shape each of us as adults and parents. The experiences of the families in the House will strike a chord with hundreds of other families who have suffered similar experiences. The important thing is to know that you are never alone with a problem – no matter how isolated you feel – and to cultivate the belief that you can change your current situation for the better.

Unresolved grief

Trauma and loss are painful to deal with and never more so than when that loss involves a parent or a child. During the course of their time in the House, several of the parents had the courage to talk to me about past grief, which they had realized was having an impact on their parenting styles. Paula, Alyson and Sara had each suffered a form of bereavement, but none of them had allowed themselves to mourn fully or move on from the experience.

'Your child will trigger memories of your own childhood.'

Inside the House

Paula's story

Surface problem: Her sons' eating disorders.

Underlying problem: Unresolved grief relating to post-natal depression.

Paula, with partner Steve, needed to work through her deep sadness at having missed out on crucial months in the lives of sons Jacob and Isaac when she was in hospital suffering from post-natal depression. (See also pages 84–5.) Her unexpressed grief had been channelled unknowingly into an extreme anxiety associated with feeding her boys. She was spoon-feeding them by hand in an unconscious desire to keep them in their baby phase so as to make up for lost time.

The turning point:

At the end of a hard-working and extraordinary week during which both her sons overcame associated eating problems, I gave Paula a framed picture of youngest son, Isaac, when he was a baby. This was a deeply painful and challenging moment for Paula, who had never been able to look at pictures of her boys as babies. She was now ready to face her fear, and recognized the importance of coming to terms with the past if she was to avoid a recurrence of her boys' eating problems in the future.

Inside the House

Alyson's story

Surface problem: Daughter Lucie's uncontrollable tantrums.

Underlying problem: Unresolved grief relating to loss of her mother, combined with split parenting style.

Alyson had a deep and traumatic memory of her mother walking out on the family with no explanation, when Alyson was just seven years old. She had transferred her deep sense of loss and abandonment onto her daughter Lucie and was convinced that Lucie suffered in the same way Alyson did each time she was separated from her. Alyson kept Lucie close to her at all times and had no control at all over her huge tantrums. As a result of her closeness to her daughter, Richard felt excluded.

The turning point

However, in a powerful family-sculpting exercise (see page 32) it became clear that Lucie adored her daddy as well as her mummy. Alyson and Richard's divided and contradictory parenting style was feeding Lucie's tantrums and encouraging her to play up. Once they took a united approach to parenting, her uncontrollable tantrums gradually came under control and the atmosphere within the family changed.

Dr Tanya says...

'If a child says, "I don't want daddy, I want mummy", it is important that mummy stands next to daddy and is able to say, with the minimum of fuss, "I have to do x, y or z at the moment; daddy's here, you go and play".'

Inside the House
Sara and Darren's story

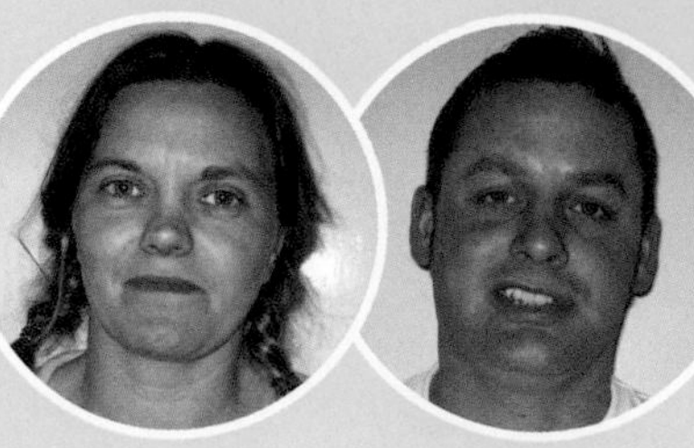

Surface problem: Son Harrison's violent outbursts.

Underlying problem: Unresolved grief relating to premature loss of their baby girl, combined with negative attitude and parenting style, and difficulty in expressing emotions.

Sara, mum to Harrison, was a vulnerable but determined woman who had never grieved for a baby daughter whom she lost late in pregnancy. At the time Harrison was born she was still carrying unresolved grief for her lost baby. Sara desperately wanted her daughter back and was unprepared for having a son, so Harrison had unwittingly disappointed her from the first moment of his birth. Darren, father to Harrison, had lost his father when he was only 7 years old. He had dealt with a lot of loss and disappointment during his life and found it hard to express his emotions. Both he and wife Sara felt they were trapped in a 'marriage of convenience' and neither felt able to show spontaneous affection to the other.

Harrison was suffering a great deal in the crossfire of the relationship and his moods changed like a highly sensitive barometer to reflect the sadness and defensiveness around him. The clues to Harrison's anxious behaviour lay in his near-phobic attitude to food and an obsessive need to keep his cars and toys in rigidly

neat and ordered rows. This was a boy who felt threatened by chaos.

The turning point

Sara acknowledged that Harrison had been wrongly labelled as a letdown from day one, and that was why she had been unable to bond with him properly. Her negative attitude was having a crushing effect on Harrison. In turn, Harrison's chronic anxiety was turning him into an aggressive and unhappy boy. I encouraged Darren and Sara to be more supportive of one another and to start to shower positive praise and to use positive practice (see page 40) on Harrison several times a day.

Sara found it hard to express warmth and affection – but as she worked hard to change her attitude towards Harrison and her husband, the positive results were a joy to see. The transformation was phenomenal. Once he felt truly loved and wanted by his parents, 'problem' child Harrison blossomed into a loving and lovely little boy whose multiple negative behaviours disappeared almost overnight.

If these stories have resonance for you or your partner and you have suffered a traumatic event in your recent or distant past, find someone whom you trust – whether a loved one, a friend or a trained professional – and talk it out. Acknowledging the issue is half the battle. Recognizing the impact it is having on your relationship or your responses as a parent can take longer to see than to resolve. (See Further Resources on page 156.)

'Facing up to the past will help to normalize past events so you can move on.'

Inside the House
Julie and Alan's story

Surface problem: Daughter Ellie's demanding behaviour.
Underlying problem: over-anxious and fearful of harm coming to their child, combined with over-indulgent parenting style and an inability to say 'no'.

Julie (mother to Ellie, aged 2) was another parent whose anxiety was displayed through excessive tidiness. In her case the concern related to fears for Ellie's safety. Having lost her father unexpectedly to a brain haemorrhage, Julie was terrified of losing her daughter in a similar or sudden way. Her concern was so extreme that she wouldn't even let Ellie attempt to walk or climb the stairs unaided and every night Ellie slept in her parents' bed.

Husband Alan was less anxious than Julie, but he was over-indulgent because he was away from home a lot. As a result he found it hard to be strict with Ellie.

We tackled Julie's fears by encouraging her to observe from afar while Ellie bounced safely on a trampoline and rode a pony. The child's delight was immense, but Julie's anxiety was clear to see, as we had fitted her up to a heart-rate monitor.

Turning point
Daughter Ellie's only moment of anxiety came when mum appeared on the scene to watch her daughter and feed the pony. Julie recoiled as the pony slobbered when she fed him an apple. Ellie immediately copied her mum and became nervous and anxious. In that moment Julie began to recognize the negative impact her own fears had on her little girl and that by holding her daughter back

from learning to take small risks, she was endangering her natural development and coping skills.

The two parents worked hard to control Ellie's tantrums and to take a healthier attitude to controlled risk. Ellie responded well to her new-found toddler status and after two nights of using the gradual withdrawal technique in the House, she was able to settle down to sleep easily by herself and in her own bed.

Seeing the world through a child's eyes

Children evoke very primitive feelings within us. When you look at your child you see the child within yourself; you see the relationship you have with your parents and, on some level, you relive past triumphs and hurts.

In the same way, when a child looks at his parents or listens to their reactions he sees the ramifications of his own actions. You are your child's world and everything you do and say has an impact upon their understanding of who they are and how they are valued.

If you have issues with your parents or extended family that remain unresolved, it is possible to get into patterns of behaviour that will repeat, in different forms, for generations.

Darren, Harrison's father, was particularly aware of this. At my final session with him and his wife Sara, he was absolutely adamant that he wanted his little boy to have a different quality of parenting and family life to the one that he himself had known.

'We're going to break the chain. I'm not going to let things go back to how they were.' (Darren)

Family sculpting

Young children often find it easier to talk about a situation by using pictures or by 'showing' rather than 'telling'. Family sculpting is a device used to encourage children to 'model' their families: whether in a drawing, for a photograph, or using dolls or other props. I used it several times in families where there was unhappiness or split parenting styles to help the parents to see family life through their children's eyes. But it can also be used in a more lighthearted and fun way; to encourage your children to express themselves and to gain insight into how they see the world.

Harrison (5 years 3 months) reduced his mum to tears when he drew a picture of her unsmiling and cross. I asked him why she looked like that. He told me it was because he is a naughty boy. I asked him how he'd like his mummy to think of him. He said 'good boy'. It was a transformational moment for both parents, as it demonstrated their son's sensitivity and challenged their view of him as a problem and a nuisance.

Drawing

Encourage your child to draw pictures of your family with the normal facial expressions. If faces look sad or angry, encourage your child to talk about how they feel about that and take steps to turn the situation around. Pay attention to the distance between each character and find out why the scene is drawn that way. Placement on the page can be very revealing.

Photographs

Turn your child into an art director and ask him or her to compose a family group for photographing. Find out why he made those decisions and what is going on beneath the surface. Don't prejudge or lead; encourage your child to express themselves in their own way.

Lucie (3 years 6 months) changed the mindset of her parents by directing her mum and dad to hold hands while she held on to her daddy's leg. Mum Alyson and dad Richard were astonished. They hadn't felt close enough to hold hands for months, and the family myth was that Lucie preferred to be with her mum.

Puppets

Use puppets or other three-dimensional figures to get your child to tell the story of your family. Ask them to tell you the story of a typical day at home, complete with voices and showing different moods and emotions. Ask questions that will encourage your little one to open up and tell you how they feel.

Kelsey (4) had quite an argumentative relationship with mum Sarah. Sarah was very concerned that she was encouraging Kelsey to grow up too fast and wanted to get closer to Kelsey. They spent a morning creating mummy and baby scarecrows. I then asked Kelsey where I should put them and what sort of face the mummy scarecrow had. She replied, 'a cross face' and directed the scarecrows to be fairly far apart. She then said that 'when mummy has a cross face, I have a cross face.' I asked her how she would like her mummy to be. She said she wished she was not cross all the time – and that she wanted a cuddle.

Split parenting

Imagine for a moment that you are your child and that you are getting mixed messages from each of your parents: one parent wants you to stop playing but the other is happy for you to continue. One parent says you can't have any more sweets, while the other slips you a few more. At best you will play one parent off against the other to gain maximum advantage; at worst you will try to please both parents and end up anxious and confused. It is hard to over-estimate the importance of having the consistent and unified involvement of both parents, if they are living together.

Several of the couples in the house had to find a way of reaching mutual ground before they could solve their parenting problems.

Inside the House

Richard and Alyson

Richard and Alyson, parents to Lucie (3 years 6 months), were emotionally distant when they arrived at the House and were no longer listening to one another's needs. Alyson could never say 'no' to Lucie, and she and Richard would overrule each other's parenting decisions. Lucie was in control of their lives and out of control with her tantrums. I focused on getting Richard more involved in parenting his daughter, while Alyson learned to spend time separately from Lucie (see page 27).

It was a hard week for them both, but once Lucie's parents began to present a united front and learned to back each other up in order to control her behaviour, she calmed down and was happier. By the end of the week, the calm and contented family they all wanted to be had started to look like an achievable reality.

Inside the House Lee and Louise

Lee and Louise, parents to Hannah (6) and Jessica (nearly 4), were also close to breaking point when they arrived at the House. Louise was permanently fraught and anxious as a result of her daughters' tantrums, while Lee was becoming an increasingly distant father. Neither of them really wanted to be in their home any more. I focused on getting them playing together as a family and encouraged Lee to take more responsibility for his girls.

Having fun became the catalyst for unifying them as a family. Once the parents began to take joint responsibility for the girls' naughty behaviour, their split parenting became a thing of the past. The girls responded well to the change and they committed to their new approach by drawing up a parenting contract (see page 41).

Anxious parenting

We all get anxious; it is a normal result of the fight or flight response to new or nerve-wracking experiences.

- 'Fight' responses include: anger, confrontation, facing the challenge 'full on'.
- 'Flight' responses include: tears, withdrawal, retreating from the challenge, denial.

If you try to work around anxiety by suppressing your responses to it, the 'symptoms' will become worse and worse. At either extreme an anxious parent may come across as 'angry' or 'unassertive'. They are opposite sides of the same coin. (See Chapter 5, Anger management and Assertiveness, pages 121–3 and 38 for more information.)

People experience anxiety in different ways, but most are likely to experience one or more of these physiological and psychological responses:

Physiological markers:

- You get hot and bothered.
- Your heart starts racing.
- You feel you might be breathing a bit quicker.
- You have increased muscle tension.
- You suffer tension headaches.
- You have a feeling of tightness across the chest.

Psychological markers:

- Automatic negative responses – 'No', 'Don't', 'It's not possible'.
- A defeatist attitude – 'I can't...', 'I never...'
- A tendency towards obsessive behaviour or elaborate rituals, e.g. around eating or tidiness.

Most of the parents in the House displayed symptoms of anxiety at one time or another; the challenge as a parent is to show your child that you are managing that anxiety. For a child, anxiety is contagious. A child's radar picks up parental anxiety more quickly than the parent himself. They may express it in different ways: through anger, through eating problems, through tantrums, or through withdrawal and shyness.

If you suspect your child is showing signs of anxiety, help them to find the words they need to describe the experience. Ask: 'Have you got a fizzy tummy?' 'Does your heart feel as if it is pounding?' 'Do your legs feel wobbly?' Depending on the age of the child, encourage them to draw or explain the source of their anxiety so that you can both understand better.

Communication

The quality of your parent–child relationship often shows in the way you speak to your child. If you feel comfortable praising and playing but find it hard to follow through with the negative consequences when you are trying to discipline them, I hope you will find Chapter 5 useful. A child who hears 'yes' and receives lots of praise and positive reinforcement will know they are loved, which is wonderful; but positive interaction also means learning the consequences of 'no' – in order to help learn self-control and understand the difference between right and wrong.

If your child's behaviour is making life a challenge, you may find that your interaction has become mainly negative. If you spend more time saying 'no', 'don't do that', 'stop it' or

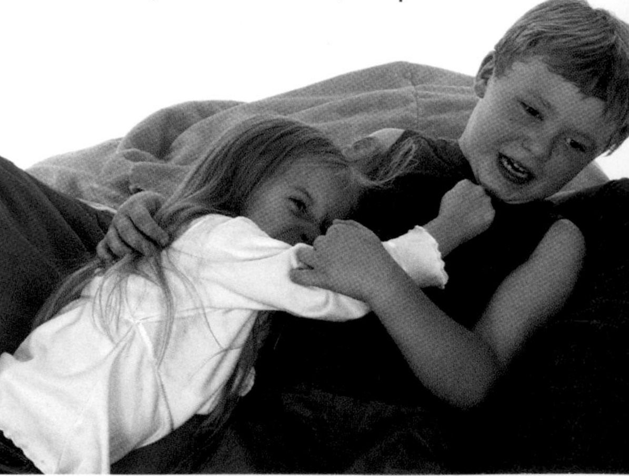

'shut up' to your child, rather than 'well done', 'tell me what you're doing', 'let's play nicely' or 'tell me about it'; you will need to increase your levels of praise and play to reassure your child and let them know you care. It will also build up positive feelings about yourself as a parent.

Negative comments have a powerful impact and lower your child's self-esteem. Think of a time when you have felt vulnerable to criticism and lacked confidence. If you received five compliments and one criticism, the chances are the criticism had a power that outweighed all the praise. That is why unconstructive criticism has no place in parenting. A young child needs help to learn from their mistakes.

Understanding anger

If your child is going through a phase that is testing your resolve and you are concerned that you may lose your temper, you need to learn to 'keep your cool' and remind yourself that you are the adult in the relationship. (See the positive belief programme on pages 42–3.) Recognize that what your child is saying and doing comes from a developing personality and that you have a responsibility for shaping their behaviour in a positive fashion.

If you are finding that your child is engaging with you in a very primitive and emotional way – not just in irritation or in anger, but in a way that is making you actively dislike them – you really have to say to yourself, 'How can I dislike someone who is really just developing and learning how to be and how to behave? What am I seeing here?' The chances are that you are seeing something about yourself that you dislike or feel uncomfortable with, which is being mirrored in your child.

If you're worried that you may lose control at some moment, get some help to manage your anger.

'Positive praise and ignoring bad behaviour go hand in hand. Neither works as well without the other.'

A self-fulfilling prophesy

'A child who is forever labelled as a troublemaker, a failure, a nuisance, a brat, or worse, will begin to 'live down' to expectations and develop low self-esteem. The message received is that they are unloved, unwanted and can do nothing right. An environment of endless criticism has a negative impact on your child as well as on your parent–child relationship.'

Being assertive

An assertive parent is a confident parent who has belief in their own abilities and will earn the respect of their child. Assertiveness is not the same as aggression: it is not about bullying or scaring your child into submission; it is about expressing your wishes in a clear and firm voice which means your child will easily understand what you want him or her to do.

- Say it as if you mean it: use an authoritative tone of voice.
- Use body language to emphasize what you are saying.
- Use facial expressions to emphasize what you are feeling.
- Open your eyes wider than usual and smile or frown to emphasize your words – depending on the mood you wish to convey.
- Don't send a mixed message: don't smile if you're angry and don't frown if you're delivering praise.
- Think to yourself, I know I can't do x, but I believe I am capable of learning and I have the confidence to be able to say to people, 'I don't know what I am doing', and don't feel embarrassed by it.

The importance of self-belief

Having belief in yourself as a worthy and able parent is central to being the strong, assertive and loving centre of your child's world. Becoming a parent is unlike any other job in life. You may be well regarded and self-assured in your professional life, or be the life and soul of the party socially, but none of that counts when life balance changes and you become a parent. Conflicting advice from friends, family and other well-meaning 'experts' can send an inexperienced or anxious parent into a tailspin. Add to that the effects of chronic sleep deprivation and the perpetual cycle of domestic chores that goes with having a young family, and is it any wonder that some parents start to doubt their ability to 'do the job'?

A parent with a low sense of self-worth will be less likely to believe they can bring about change. For that reason, I do a lot of work that focuses on building parental confidence and reframing personal beliefs.

Self-esteem

Self-esteem is a foundation stone of self-belief. Self-esteem represents 'what I believe about myself'. To have high self-esteem means to hold an inbuilt positive belief about your self – it doesn't mean that you are confident all the time, but that you hold the belief that you will adjust to a situation or learn to cope.

Self-esteem goes hand in hand with assertiveness. It is a critical quality for confident parenting because it will enable you to have the self-belief to 'hold fast' when your little one is challenging your every move, and will give you the resilience to stay objective and keep things in perspective – especially when your toddler starts hurling personal abuse! (See page 42.)

Can you change a child's self-esteem? Definitely. Sara and Darren (Harrison's parents), are proof of that. Harrison arrived at the House playing up and sobbing by turn; by the time they left there were more smiles than tears. Kisses, cuddles and lots of positive attention transformed him.

The leap of faith

Single mum Nicola was feeling depressed and her belief in herself as a parent was extremely low. Nicola needed an assignment that would boost her confidence – fast! We sent her, with a close and trusted friend, to an outward-bound centre. She was terrified and convinced that she couldn't do any of it. There, in the cold and the wind, she climbed a wooden pole the height of a four-storey building, stood up, wobbled, screamed – and then leapt towards a flying trapeze.

That single act re-framed the way Nicola thought about herself and gave her the boost she needed to believe that she could be a good mum, a strong mum, and could turn Dante's behaviour around – even when she got back home.

'If you know yourself to be lacking in self-confidence, or if your self-esteem is low, get some coaching or some help to strengthen your resolve.'

Use positive practice

Several times a day, for no reason at all, go up to your child and say, 'Let me give you a kiss and a cuddle – because I love you. It doesn't have to be in response to them doing anything special, but just because they *are*.

Dr Tanya says...
'Several times a day, for no reason at all, go up to your child and say, "Let me give you a kiss and a cuddle – because I love you."'

Ladle on the praise

Imagine you have a large bucket and ladle in every room, and that bucket contains praise – in whatever form you imagine it to be. Make a conscious effort to get that ladle out as often as you can and pour praise over your child; but do it with enthusiasm and sincerity so your child really feels the integrity of what you are saying as well as hearing the words. Praise can lose its meaning if it is insincere or used indiscriminately.

Be expressive

If you are praising your child, smile as you speak and open your eyes wide. The 'bigness' of what you say will emphasize your meaning.

Use incentives

Sticker charts and other incentives can be used to help your child to understand their behaviour and to see their own progress. (See page 112.)

If your child is being overly wilful and you need practical guidelines to curb naughty behaviour, please use the guidelines laid out in the good behaviour programme on page 125.

Use positive interaction

Improving the quality of the interaction you have with your child will work

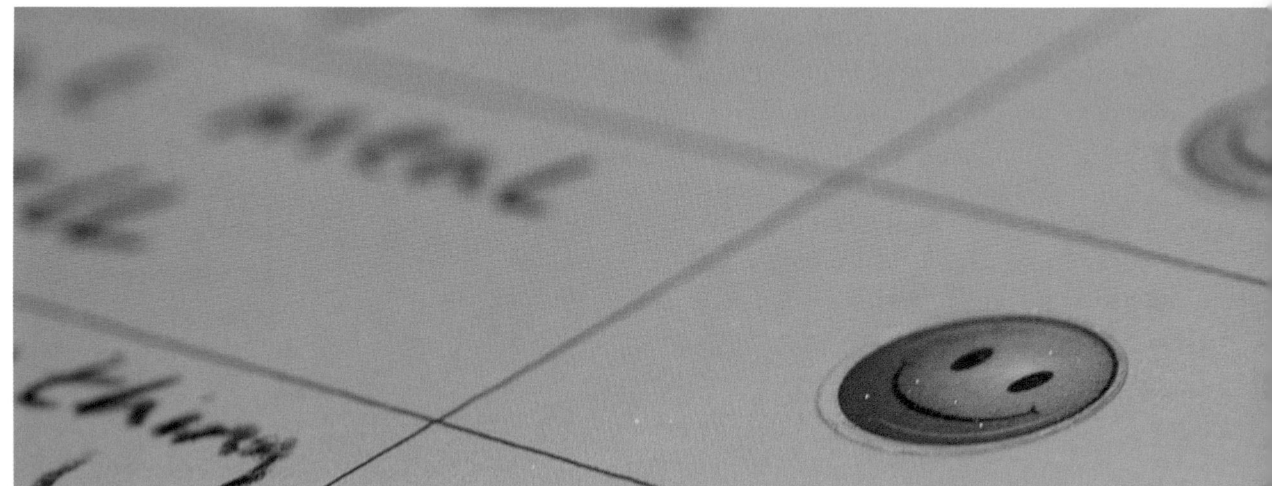

wonders for your relationship and lead to a lot more fun and laughter for your family. Positive interaction can be verbal or non-verbal, physical or mental; it is to do with communicating positively with your child and being conscious of the messages you are giving to him or her.

Give your children your time

Our modern lives are lived much too fast and with a complex set of conflicting priorities and jam-packed schedules. If you feel that work is taking over your life and you are missing out on playtime with your kids, plan ahead to spend quality time with them – put dates in the diary that are sacrosanct and really 'boot up' the level of positive interaction you have with your child.

Enjoy playtime

Play with your children, 'attend' to their progress and take the time to encourage their activity (see page 59). Play and praise are the subject of the next chapter and, together with parenting skills, they are the cornerstones of positive parenting.

Planning the future

As the saying goes, 'If you keep doing what you're doing, you'll keep getting what you've got.' In other words, if you want things to be different, something has to change. I hope that this book will help you enhance or transform the relationship you have with your child.

Many of the parents, especially those who had trouble seeing eye to eye, were given the task of preparing a parenting contract. The contract can be used in different ways: as a contract between you and your partner, or as a contract between you and your children. It doesn't need to be complex, but should lay down your commitment to change negative behaviours, set boundaries, to play and to praise. The Turner family contract was drawn up by 6-year-old Hannah.

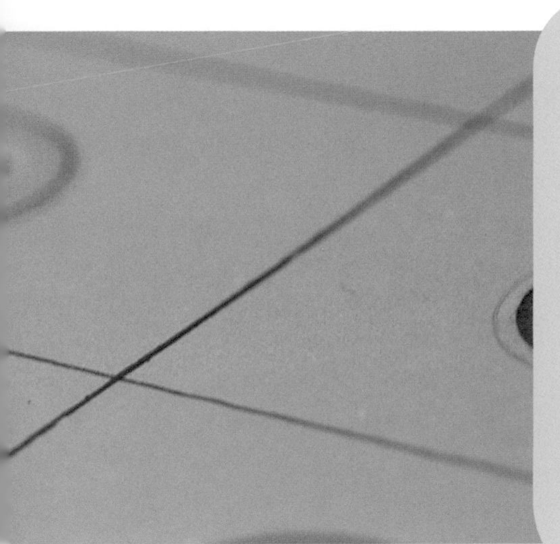

The Turner Family Contract

Mum and Dad
1. Play more at home.
2. Don't shout.
3. Stop smacking.
4. More cuddles and kisses.

Hannah and Jessica
1. Play much more.
2. Play nicely.
3. Wait until mum and dad stop talking.

Lee and Louise framed their contract when they returned home and it is referred to on a regular basis.

The following chapters provide clear guidelines on playing and praising your child, as well as coping with a range of behavioural problems: from eating and sleep problems to tantrums, aggression and wilful behaviour in public. Each chapter includes a parenting programme that summarizes the key points in the chapter and gives you positive strategies for behaviour-shaping.

The positive belief programme which follows offers you positive self-management tools to increase your confidence as a parent and reshape your beliefs about yourself and your child.

Dr Tanya's positive belief programme

Commit to your child

Enhance your parent–child relationship by focusing on the following essentials:

- Love your child and praise them frequently so that they feel valued and wanted.
- Set clear boundaries so that your child knows where they stand.
- Provide them with clear routines and structure so that they feel safe and know what to expect.
- Be consistent in your approach so that they learn the behaviour well.
- Reward your child for being good, trying hard or doing well to build their self-esteem.
- Follow through with clear consequences if they misbehave, so that they learn from their mistakes.
- Give them cuddles and affection at every opportunity so that they know they are loved.

Increase your assertiveness

An assertive parent is a confident parent who has belief in their own abilities and will earn the respect of their child:

- Use an authoritative tone of voice to rein in your child's bad behaviour.
- Use body language to emphasize praise.
- Use facial expressions to emphasize what you are feeling.
- Take steps to build your confidence if your self-esteem is low.
- Get help to manage your anger if you fear you could lose control.

Anger management

- Distract yourself by counting or singing to yourself to take your mind off your annoyance.
- Put a barrier between yourself and what you are experiencing.
- If you feel you are going to blow, remove yourself from the room until you have regained control.
- Remember that if you start to shout and fill your child's head with negative thoughts, your words will reinforce the

negative behaviour.

- Look for support.

Learn to relax

- Control your breathing by slowing it down and breathing from your diaphragm.
- Focus on relaxing your muscles; chances are that your brow is furrowed, your neck is hunched, your shoulders are high and taut and your fists may be clenched. You're in anxious mode.
- Think about the non-verbal message that you're giving to your child. If they can see you are anxious, they will become anxious too.
- Don't expect too much from yourself.

Monitor your own behaviour

- Are you being negative? Do you suffer from anxiety?
- Take action to get yourself into a different frame of mind.
- Choose to feel happy.
- Begin a behaviour diary and monitor what kind of impact your approach is having on your child.
- Take positive steps to change your behaviour.

Not in front of the children

- A parent who is able to self-manage their moods and behaviour will be a more positive influence on their child than one who loses control easily. Children often believe themselves to be the cause of parental anguish.
- Try not to argue in front of young children – you will frighten them.
- If you do argue, let them see you make up.
- Avoid crying or losing control in front of young children – it will alarm them. Instead, remove yourself from the room with an excuse.
- Be calm and relaxed around food and make sure meals are eaten in a stress-free environment.
- Take a unified approach to parenting with your partner or family.

Draw up a parenting contract

- List the positives: what you commit to.
- List the negatives: things that are banished.
- Ask your children what they want.
- Pin it up somewhere where everyone can see it.
- Take it seriously and commit to keeping the pledge.

'The most effective parenting comes from the heart. You have to really believe in what you are doing.'

999
999

2

The Power of Play and Praise

Play is an immensely powerful parenting tool. The value of play is that it allows parents to bond with their children in an intimate and positive way that enriches everyone involved. Children learn about themselves and others through play; they develop their cognitive and creative skills and their understanding of the world about them.

Many parents show surprise when they come to me to explain how disruptive and naughty their child is, only to be told they need to play with them more. The more time you are able to spend playing with your child, the less time your child will have to think up ways to express their need for attention by more negative behaviour. Positive play encourages children to take responsibility for their own actions, whilst also involving the parent.

The power of play

Child's play is essential for knowledge and a good way to develop:

- a close bond with you as a parent.
- sharing and social skills.
- cognitive skills and the imagination.
- individuality – through role play and experimentation.

And also to learn:

- physical as well as reasoning skills.
- who they are and what they enjoy.
- how to take risks in a safe environment.

It also expends energy that could otherwise be channelled into more destructive behaviour. Most importantly, it encourages children to laugh and have fun.

Inside the House Lee, Louise, Hannah (6 years), Jessica (3 years 8 months)

'It's got to the stage ... that if we don't resolve something with the kids... we could end up splitting up for a while.'

The home of Lee and Louise had become a battleground. Jessica's daily temper tantrums were aggressive, and quality family time was a thing of the past. Louise had put her career on hold to become a full-time mum. Her life revolved around Jessica and Hannah. Her partner Lee missed most of the tantrums whilst at work.

From the outset I was struck by how anxious the parents were, and how negative they were towards their children. In the first ten minutes in the House they said 'No' to the girls nearly once every 20 seconds. When the girls did something lovely, they got no feedback. While Louise policed their behaviour, Lee held back.

There was a really sad atmosphere in the family: the parents felt that their relationship was on the verge of breaking up and the children had little self-control. Although the problem appeared to be the children's behaviour, the real problem lay in Lee and Louise's split parenting and their inability to praise or play with their children. Louise felt foolish at the idea of letting herself go, but her daughters, and Lee, soon put her straight. By being encouraged to be silly, Louise gained confidence in her ability to play with her girls.

Their commitment to learning new skills was a great success, and by day six a real joy had replaced the sadness.

Making time to play

Many modern parents are time-starved and under pressure. They find that they have little time to make their child an evening meal, let alone play with them. If you feel that you are spending more time cooking and cleaning than playing with your child, then think forward to when he or she has grown up and ask yourself, what are they more likely to remember – the meals you put on the table, or the fun you had and the games you used to play?

Preparing meals is the perfect time to bond with your child. Cooking together, preparing vegetables, mixing and mashing are all great fun for kids – and they won't need separate supervision either.

Playtime is fun – for both adults and children – and I'm here to tell you that it comes first; ahead of cooking, cleaning, washing-up, making phone calls and shopping! Turn chores into play and learning opportunities. Play is a way to teach your child life skills, too. Give yourself permission to enjoy your child, and for them to enjoy you, too.

'Playing will help you to get to know your child better.'

Young children need and relish your attention; they seek it in many and varied ways every day. No matter how overwhelmed you are feeling about other aspects of your life, scheduling time to play with your child in a positive way will reap great rewards when it comes to creating the behaviour you would like at other times.

Children enjoy attention

If young children don't receive a positive response to positive actions they will try and get a response by seeking your attention in other ways – such as by playing up, hitting, screaming or crying. There were many moments in the House when creative play transformed tears into laughter; stopped a tantrum before it had begun and defined moments where a parent began to bond positively with their child in a new way.

Don't be afraid to let your child feel bored occasionally. It will help them to learn to manage downtime. Life is not always about constant stimulation.

Dr Tanya says...

'If you make time to play with your kids you will find they are the best stress-buster ever.'

O Verbal rewards are shown by using your voice with varied expression and enthusiasm.
O Non-verbal rewards are shown using body language, eye contact and touch – including hugs.

An effective way of playing with your child that allows them to manage their own activities and to develop their own strengths – while also bonding and learning from you – is by attending to and rewarding your child as they play. This takes the form of actively engaging with your child and commenting on your child's play.

Rewarding, as it suggests, means giving praise and encouragement to your child in both verbal and non-verbal ways. The important thing is to allow your child to lead the play so that they are in control of the action and learning to express themselves – without interference.

Don't take control of the game – and don't be tempted to tell them what they should do, or how they should play it. They lead – you follow. They need to be able to learn from their progress and their mistakes. Rewarding is not about giving a child lavish gifts or about getting the activity perfectly 'right'; it is about parent–child bonding and making time for and getting to know your child.

Paying attention to your child and their needs and rewarding them for good or positive and creative behaviour, allows them to know that you are there and to feel safe while learning through play. If you show them respect for who they are and what they do, you will get the same back in return.

Let them lead

Play the part of a commentator and encourage your child to pretend to be a dancer/ score a winning goal in a ball game/ take off in a spacecraft. Let them lead the action, but in your role as commentator describe with enthusiasm what your child is doing at every stage and reward them with praise for their manoeuvres.

'Jonny is putting the car into first gear, now up to second, and third... *[What a clever boy he is.]* Now he is driving down the straight. *[Look how fast he is going. Well done Jonny. Go, go, go!]* And what's he doing now? Jonny's facing the challenge of putting the car into the pit stop. Can he do it? It's a difficult angle but, yes, he can. *[Perfect. A great result.]* At this rate he'll soon be winning the Grand Prix!

Make precious time to play with your children – and you won't be disappointed. Apart from developing a closer bond, you will be amazed, amused and delighted by the things your kids say and do. They have wonderful originality and, if you give them your positive attention, they are the best stress-busters ever.

'Group play is fun and a great way to see how children think and interact.'

I often use play to find out how families get along together. Creating a family drawing will tell you a lot about how your child thinks and feels and will build a bond between you, too. But play isn't just for children. It helps parents to relax and express themselves. 'Before' and 'after' collages drawn in the House were very revealing and showed how feelings changed from negative to positive during the course of the week.

Relax and play

Not every parent finds playing with their children easy to do.

It might have been many years since you really let yourself go in a silly or madcap way, so if you find that you feel inhibited and unable to free up your imagination – adopt a different persona for the occasion! Be someone else for an hour. In time you will lose your shyness and reconnect with your creative and playful side.

I often say to parents, imagine you are a children's party entertainer and are wound up to high speed. Be crazy, be silly; let yourself go. Your children will love it.

Play doesn't have to be educational all the time – it doesn't always have to be about doing jigsaws and reading books. Play is about rolling around on the floor; it's about physical contact; it's about having a really good laugh together. Playtime is the time for you to make contact with your child in a way that gives you both pleasure. It is about your child recognizing that you enjoy being with them. It's an incredibly powerful experience.

During the course of each week in the House it was noticeable that the level of noise seemed to stay the same, but the type of noise changed – as children shifted from tantrums and screaming in frustration, to shouting in good spirits. Equally, the parents' behaviour was transformed from complaining to praising; tears transformed into laughter. Laughter is an incredible force for good; it is immensely exciting to see how willing children are to be happy. Laughter releases natural endorphins into the body that lift the mood – so child's play is therapeutic for you, too.

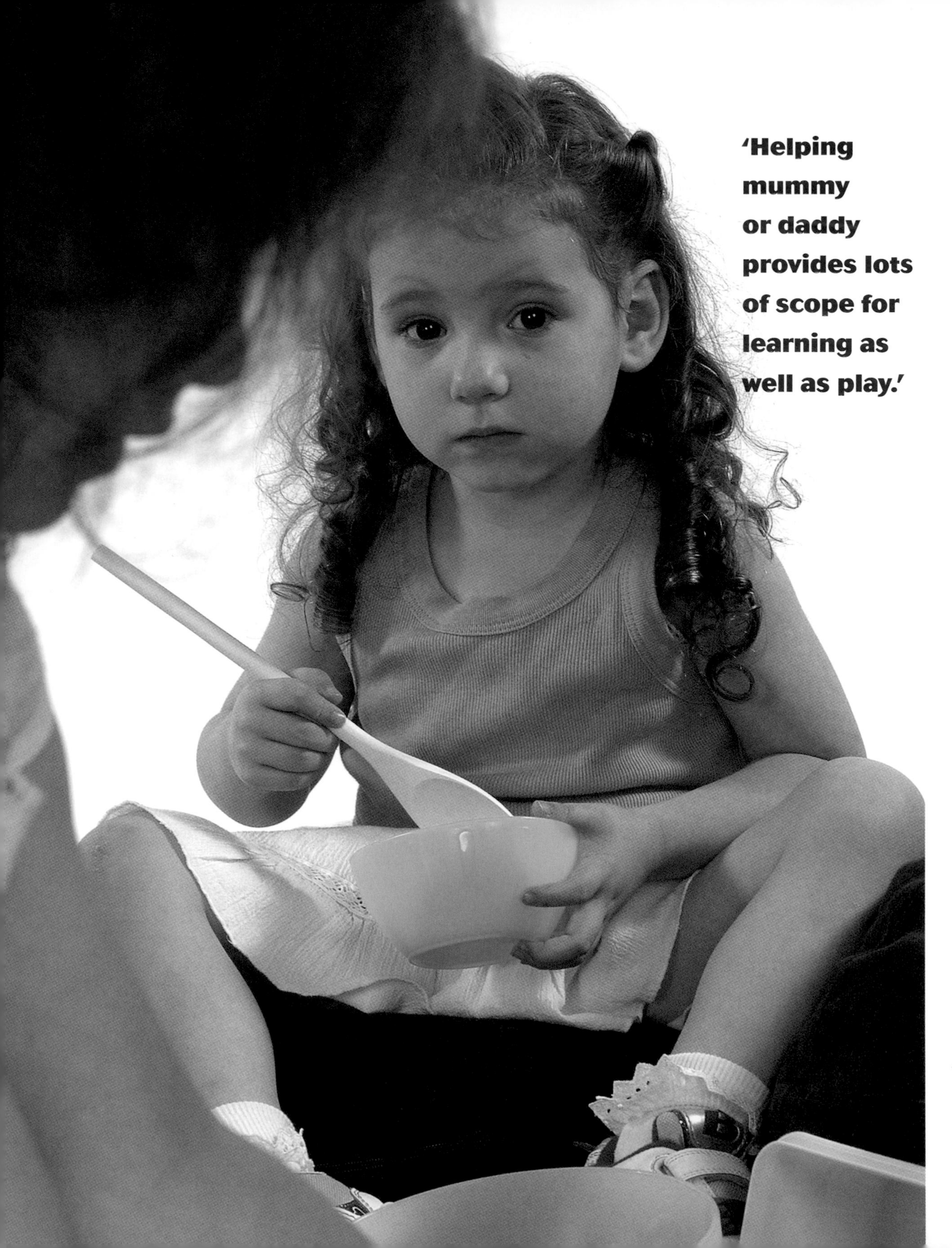

'Helping mummy or daddy provides lots of scope for learning as well as play.'

Learning through play

Many children have dozens of toys that they never play with. Parents do not always encourage them to play with them either. Abandon electronic toys, turn off the TV and find other ways of entertaining your child. Experiment with simple, everyday items and encourage your child to use their imagination to create a world of play.

Don't worry about children needing to 'act their age' when they play – it can be really nice for older children to play as they would when they were younger from time to time. It's a way of recontacting a different part of themselves.

- Provide tins and packets of food from the cupboard and see how long it takes for a game of 'shop' to evolve.
- Get out a cardboard box and see how quickly it can become a play box – for hide and seek, playing at being a postman, hiding things, or even becoming a sledge.
- Give your child a saucepan, a container of water and a wooden spoon to play with and he or she will quickly use them in an imaginative game.
- Give them a sheet or a blanket and allow them to create a 'den' out of household furniture.

The joy and laughter will be well worth the resulting mess!

Make shopping a game

The idea of combining children and shopping is many parents' idea of hell. The fear of losing control of their children, the embarrassment of facing a tantrum in public and the utter carnage that a wilful toddler can cause in a matter of minutes is enough to strike fear in the heart of many a robust adult. (It might also send them to shop via the internet in future, rather than risk leaving home.)

Children play up when they are bored. If their environment is over-controlled or lacking in stimulation, they are likely to create their own entertainment. The answer is to make shopping a team effort, and to make it fun.

Try some of the suggestions in the list below: they might not alter your child's behaviour overnight, but you will be taking a positive step in the right direction.

- Play 'I-spy' to encourage your youngsters to help you find what you need.
- Take labels from food cartons with you to the shops so that toddlers can learn to recognize colours and shapes, and can help you with your shopping.
- Ask him or her – how many red things can you spot in this aisle?
- See how fast you can make it down each aisle while loading the trolley with the items you need.
- Challenge them: who can get the peas first?

The more fun your child is having, the less likely they will be to play up because they are enjoying themselves and having a laugh.

Tips and tactics for managing more than one child:

Set up some friendly competition by seeing:

- who can be quiet for the longest.
- who can spot the most products with animals/people/ cartoon characters on the labels.
- how many products have coloured 'special offer' tabs.
- Whether each child can make up a story involving other people in the store.

In all cases:

- Encourage good behaviour with the promise of a (small) treat.
- Discourage bad behaviour by giving an initial warning and then ignoring the child.
- In extreme circumstances, use time out techniques. (See page 134 for guidance on how to use 'time out' in public.)

Don't do it! [Do it!]

There is a wonderful technique that I find is particularly effective. Its official description is 'paradoxical intervention' but you may find it easier to think of it as *'Don't Do It! [Do it!]'*

The idea is that you tell the child that you don't want them to do something, in order to get them to do it. The method was a great success in getting Harrison (5) to start to overcome his food anxiety.

You: (Quickly, and in a silly voice)	Child's response:
'I do not want you to eat your sandwich.'	*Giggly laughter!*
'Do not eat your sandwich!'	*Bites sandwich.*
'The last thing I want you to do is eat that sandwich!'	*More laughter!*
'Do not eat that sandwich!'	*Finishes sandwich.*

Your child will understand the joke and will also respond to your tone of voice. The rebellion is understood to be allowed and funny – but it also achieves the desired result. (It works well with adults, too!)

Children need to let off steam. Energetic play keeps kids strong and healthy, builds confidence and uses up excess energy, too. Kids love to bounce! Little Ellie used up lots of energy jumping on her first trampoline. She slept soundly that night because she was physically exhausted. A real bonus for her parents, Alan and Julie!

A child's individuality

Every child is unique and has his or her own character – their own way of expressing themselves. Play is a wonderful means of getting to know your child's nature and abilities as they develop.

Be aware of the relationship that you have with each of your children. If one child is more demanding than another it can be very easy to focus more attention on the extrovert child – whether for positive or negative reasons. By using the guidelines suggested in my creative play programme on page 59, and by referring to Chapter 7: Techniques for Taming Tearaways, you will be well-armed to treat each of your kids equally and to encourage them to develop their individuality.

Children's roles

It is quite common for an older child to be cast in the role of mini-parent and expected to set an example and to look after the younger children. It is common and understandable behaviour, but it is never fair as it casts the older child in a different role to his or her siblings.

Be conscious of how you relate to your children, and swap their roles on a regular basis. All children need equal levels of attention.

For example:

- Let younger children have a go at choosing an activity and 'go first', otherwise this can sometimes become the exclusive domain of the oldest child.
- Older children should be free to play without additional responsibility.
- The middle child needs to be put centre stage if their needs are sometimes overlooked.

If you're faced with playing with a group of children together, engage them in a shared activity, such as telling a story. Create a scenario and then encourage each child to come up with a silly storyline that will keep the tale moving:

You: *'Once upon a time there were three gorillas...'*
Child 1: *'The oldest one eats 125,000 bananas for breakfast every day and always wears red socks – because his feet get cold.'*
Child 2: *'The youngest gorilla was kidnapped by the circus when he was small but is grown up now! He eats 100 million bananas each day.'*
Child 3: *'The third one is called Mrs Banana – but she doesn't really like bananas.'*
Child 1: *'One day Red Sock discovered he had been given a magic telephone banana and so he decided to phone his friends...'*

By injecting fun into an activity you will engage all the chidren, whatever their ages.

Make it large

Your tone of voice, your facial expression, the level of enthusiasm in your voice: all these factors combine to convey a clear message to your child.

If you never change your tone of voice a child will find it hard to know whether you are happy, sad, angry or pleased about something he or she has done.

- Practise changing your facial expressions to show emotion.
- Use your body to show how you feel.
- Change your tone of voice so that the child understands whether you are happy or sad, angry or calm, proud or despairing.
- Exaggerate your gestures to reinforce your words.

Playtime ideas for parents

- **Do messy play – with water, paints, mud, food.**
- **Sing songs and make up silly verses.**
- **Say: 'Do you know what happened to me today? – and then make up a story.**
- **Create imaginary characters.**
- **Turn your child's toothbrush into a 'tooth-monster bug-zapper' and the bath sponge into a 'superclean suds machine'. This will encourage the job of cleaning teeth and washing much more effectively than raising your voice.**
- **Let your child put make-up on you – and on themselves.**
- **Let them dress up in some of your clothes.**
- **Lie on the ground together and look at the sky. Imagine pictures in the clouds.**
- **Camp out in the back garden – by hanging a sheet over the washing line.**

Children love to dress up and it encourages self-expression and imagination, too. Creating a family play is a great excuse to have fun together. Alex and Toney wrote a House play to involve all the families, which gave Harrison, Kelsey, Tobi and Tiimu the perfect excuse for face-painting.

Role play and imagination

Role play with children works wonderfully. Children love to adopt the role of teacher, shopkeeper, fireman, soldier, builder or nurse at the drop of a hat – and they can play for hours, absorbed in their imaginary world. Children need time and space to use their imaginations and to explore different worlds and identities. It is perfectly possible for a small boy to head off on his tricycle 'to work' and to return home 'in the evening' with a fascinating account of what he has been doing all day. Many a child can be found in the garden 'digging to Australia' because they have just learned that it is on the other side of the world.

Kids are amazing – they have so much to say. But in order to hear them, we need to give them our time, commit to playtime and to be non-directive in our approach and collaboration.

The power of positive praise

Praise enriches, encourages and motivates. It is the equal and opposite of criticism, and just as powerful. Take every opportunity to praise your child: be enthusiastic, say what you mean, and make sure they know that you mean what you say. Praise that is backed up by cuddles and kisses reinforces the message and will build your bond more strongly.

Be conscious of how and when you use praise. Avoid giving mixed messages, for example by saying 'good girl' or softening your tone whilst in the middle of setting a boundary or putting a child in time out. Instead, use it to great effect once the child has apologized or has taken on board what they have done wrong.

Children are like a barometer that registers the atmospheric pressure in your household and in your relationship with your partner. Almost every child in the House was an example of this, and many of the positive transformations related to the fact that key issues in the story of the parents' lives and relationship had been addressed and were closer to being resolved. (See Chapter 1.)

'Children learn a lot from each other when playing.'

Small children may not have the reasoning skills to fully understand what is going on in your life, but they have the sensitivity to know when something is not right and are very likely to think that it is them that have caused the problem in some way.

Parents need praise, too

The good practices that we are introducing to our children work well for parents, too. Have you had a hard day? Give yourself a treat. Did you manage your child's tantrum in the supermarket without losing your cool? Congratulations. Tell yourself you're great.

Make sure you and your partner support one another and make time for each other. Ok, the children cried for an hour tonight – but it was two hours last night. You have made progress. Reward yourself. Take time to reconnect with who you are as an adult and as an individual. Life is not just about your role as a parent.

Dr Tanya's creative play programme

Use different styles of play

- Messy play is a way of freeing your child from anxiety and letting off steam.
- Non-directed play allows your child to explore their own way of doing things and to find their 'voice'.

Attend to what your child is doing

- Let your child take control of play – rather than telling them what they should do, and how they should play the game.
- Show them how to develop a new skill, but try not to fuss.
- Let your child lead. You should follow.

Comment on their progress

- Pay attention to your child by commenting on their progress and rewarding them for good or positive and creative behaviour. This allows them to know that you are there and to feel safe while learning through play.
- Remember that children need to be allowed to progress by learning from their mistakes. Life is not about being 'right' 100 per cent of the time.

Reward their actions through praise and encouragement

- Give your child positive feedback – especially if they haven't got an activity 'right' first time.
- Use hugs and kisses as positive affirmation that you are enjoying playing with your child.
- Show your child respect. Remember: if you show them respect for who they are and what they do – you will get the same back in return.

Be creative

- Encourage your child to use their imagination by being 'off-the-wall' with story-telling and absurd in your suggestions.
- Involve your child in the creative process and don't dominate or modify their ideas.
- Add variety to your activities – and vary the locations where you play. Go outside and get some fresh air. It doesn't matter if it's raining, snowing or blowing. Banish predictability from playtime!

Communicate enthusiasm

- Use your whole body to communicate with your child.
- Use your voice boldly.
- Open your eyes widely.
- Smile and laugh as much as possible.

Plan your time

- Set up dedicated play times with your child.
- Making regular time to be together with your child will help you to stay in touch with their development, to deepen your personal bond, and to have special shared experiences.

Have fun!

- Playtime is for adults too – and it's precious.
- Enjoy every moment you have with your small person. You will both remember these times for years to come.

Peaceful Nights and Plenty of Sleep

There are times in every parent's life when the promise of a good night's sleep seems an impossible dream. Sleep deprivation may be an essential fact of life when your baby is newly born, but there's a danger that inappropriate sleep patterns begun at an early age will become a hard habit to break.

I find it interesting that the majority of parents who come to me for advice on sleeping problems have unwittingly given the power and responsibility for the problem to their child. They don't realize that they are responsible for teaching their child good sleep behaviour.

'He takes at least 2 hours to settle.'

'He will only fall asleep in my bed.'

'She has never slept through the night.'

Sleep problems are sometimes the root cause of behaviour problems in young children, but poor sleep habits are rarely the result of a neurological disorder. Every little body has a vital biological need to sleep, to ensure healthy cognitive, physical and neurological development. However, a lot of kids behave badly because they are quite simply tired out and parents aren't aware of how much sleep a child actually needs.

Behaviour such as waking in the night, refusing to go to sleep in their own bed, or an outright refusal to settle, are, nine times out of ten, the result of a loving parent inadvertently introducing poor sleep habits. These are often set up at an early age.

There are generally three categories of sleep problem:

- Your child can't settle himself or herself to sleep.
- Your child can't sleep through the night without waking.
- If you are unlucky – both of the above.

Sleep facts

Sleep is essential for the healthy development of your child.

By the ages of 6–12 months a child in a healthy sleep routine will be able to go to sleep on their own in a dark or dimly-lit room and will be able settle themselves back to sleep when they wake in the night.

A healthy sleep routine will allow you space away from your child and give you time to be in adult company; ensuring quality time for yourself, to be with your partner or to spend with friends.

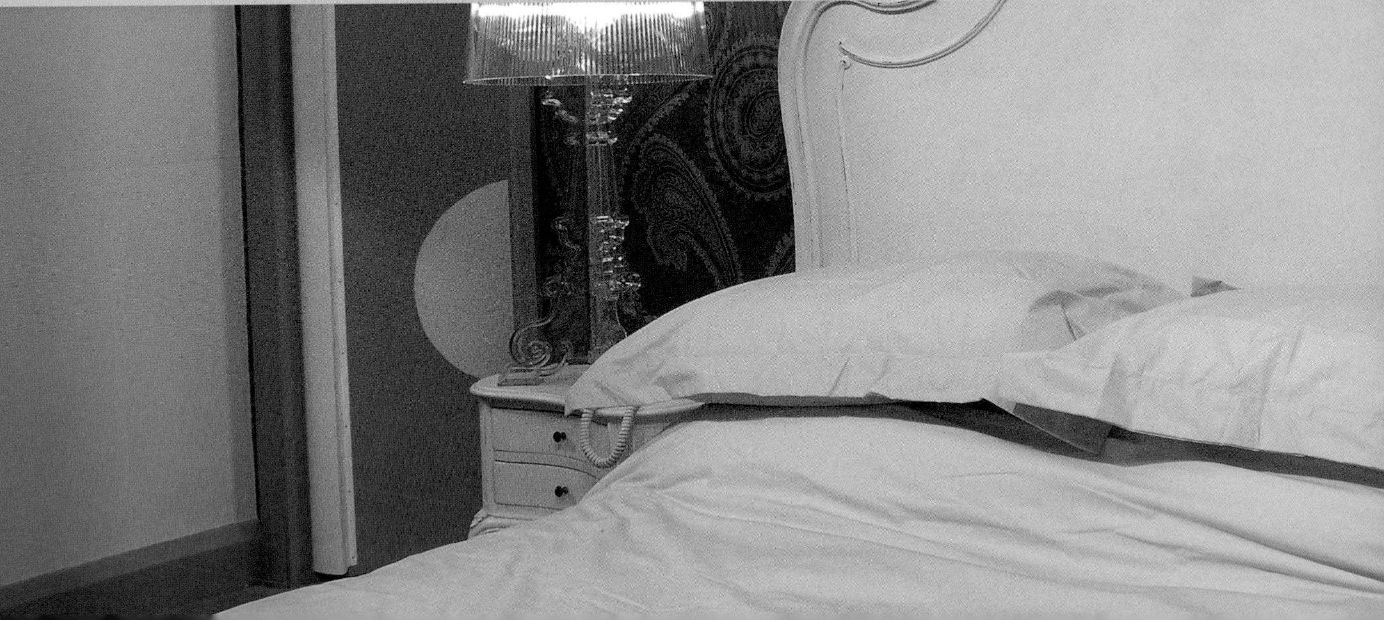

Dr Tanya says...
'If turning around the behaviour of your little one takes longer than a week – don't worry, this is normal. I was as surprised as the parents at the accelerated rate of change that took place in the House. Every child and every family is different, so be patient, be consistent and stay calm – and you will succeed.'

In reality, it is always the parent who leads and drives the child's behaviour. That may be difficult to believe if you are chronically tired and wearied by your child's insomniac behaviour and feel you have tried everything. The good news is that a healthy sleep routine can rectify poor sleep habits quite quickly and the benefits for the whole family are immense.

'Late nights and lack of sleep can lead to behaviour problems during the day.'

The impact of sleep deprivation

A young child who is developing healthily needs, and should be getting, about 11 hours of sleep per night. A child who gets by consistently on less than 8 hours per night is in a massive state of sleep deprivation. That is going to have an impact on his or her behaviour, as well as on your responses. Part of the reason several of the children in the House were so badly behaved is because they were exhausted. For many of the parents, the key word they needed to learn during their week with me was, 'No!'

Always remember that every child is different. What worked for your friend's children may not work for yours. Be patient, consistent, and if you find the behaviour is getting worse in the short term, please bear in mind that lasting behaviour change takes time to establish. With your commitment, things *will* improve, given time.

Inside the House Nicola and Dante (23 months)

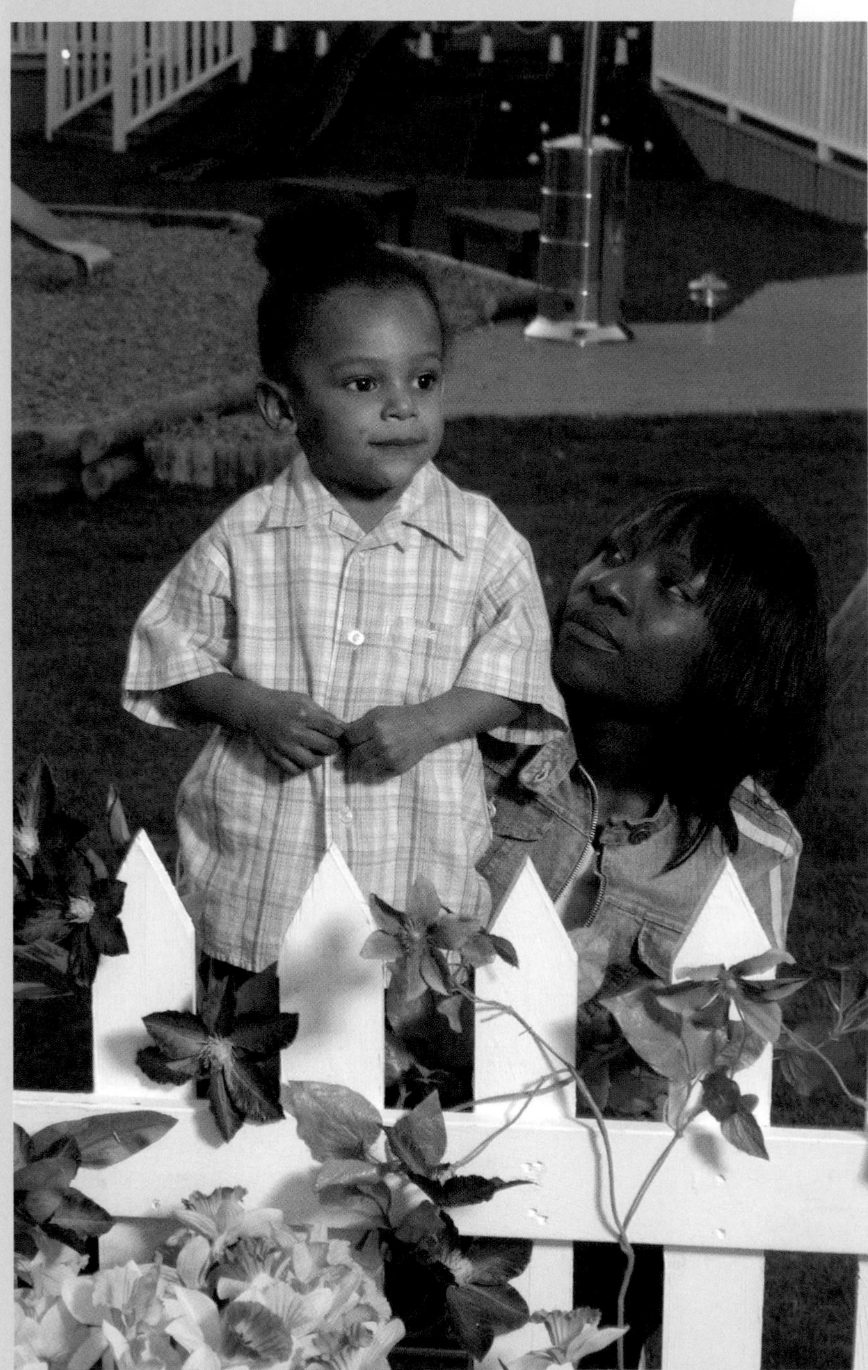

What was the problem? – Dante wouldn't go to sleep or stay in his own bed. He insisted on sleeping in Nicola's. In desperation, it got to the point where she slept on the sofa.

When did the problem start? – At birth.

Why did it happen? – Inappropriate sleep cues.

What had she tried in the past? – Nicola has a very emotional relationship with Dante and would plead with him to sleep.

Whose problem was it?
After discussion, Nicola came to realize that the problem was hers rather than Dante's. In fact, Dante was a healthy little boy, developing normally, who was responding to his mother's behaviour. Nicola was struggling with depression in her role as single mum and lacked self-confidence. As a result she had elevated Dante – at almost 2 years old – to the role of man of the house.

What did she do to keep the problem going?
Nicola's need for comfort was leading her to give in to Dante's demands and to check on him frequently when he slept. She had a tendency to reinforce his night-waking unnecessarily by bringing him hot milky drinks, and she gave him more attention than he needed at night.

How committed was she to solving the problem?
The answer was 'very' – although initially she lacked confidence in her ability to succeed. She was also aware that she could be tempted back into her old ways at times when she was feeling low or was particularly tired.

'From birth until now he hasn't had a full night's sleep, and I haven't had a full night's sleep.'

Was she willing to change her behaviour?
Nicola put in a lot of work to address her issues of low self-esteem, and worked hard to change Dante's sleep cues; making his bedroom a special place that he could enjoy and call his own. I taught her to use the rapid return technique consistently if Dante awoke and got out of bed in the night. The positive impact was clear from the first night.

The result?
The steady progress on Dante's sleep graph speaks for itself. From night one when she got him to bed at 7pm and he got up 12 times until night six when he slept through the night unaided; the Nicola and Dante story was a great success.

'Being a single parent can be tough, and it can be lonely. If you're feeling down, or in need of comfort, don't be tempted to wake or cuddle your baby in the night. If you are lonely – phone a friend.'

Inside the House Michelle, Ross (2 years 2 months) and Matthew (3 years 6 month

'I feel it's all my fault. I didn't do a routine at the beginning ... It's just that you fall into a trap and it gets worse and worse and you can't get out of it.'

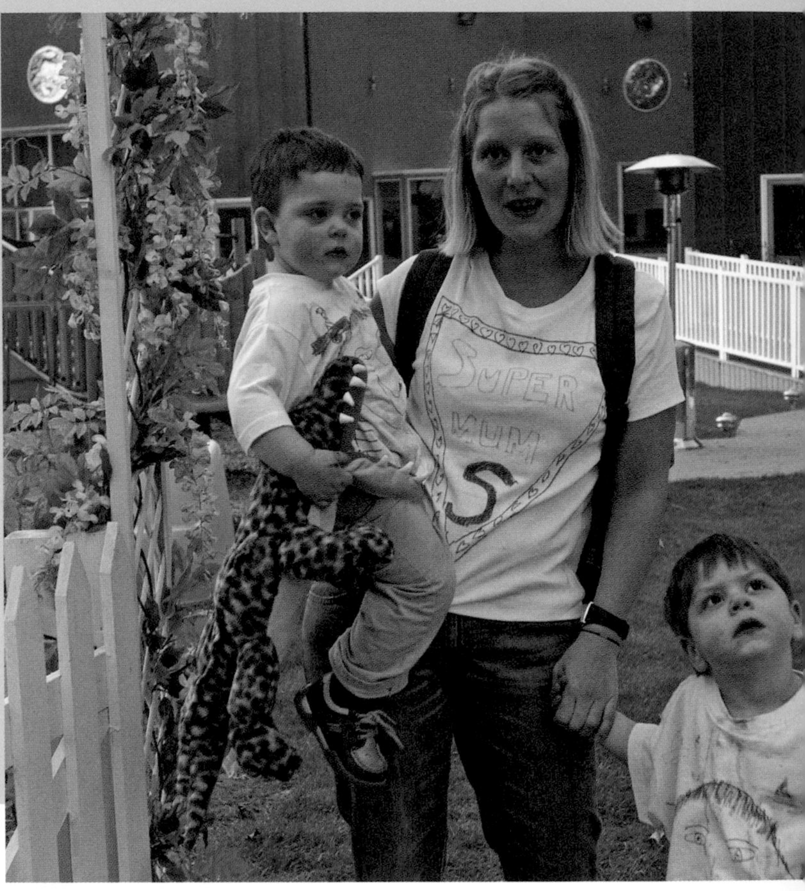

Two-year-old Ross and three-year-old brother Matthew's refusals to sleep through the night meant that Michelle hadn't had an undisturbed night's sleep since Ross was born. Their constant wakings had made every day and night a living nightmare.

What was the problem? – Chronic sleep deprivation was leading to problematic daytime behaviour in the two boys – and Michelle's exhaustion had taken her to breaking point.
When did the problem start? – Michelle felt it dated back to Ross's birth when Matthew first started to wake up during the night.
Why did it happen? – The lack of routine, and Michelle's lack of assertiveness all combined to make the situation worse.

What had she tried in the past? – Michelle had spent her nights comforting and cajoling her boys back to sleep and had learned to survive on as little as 3 hours' sleep per night.
Was it agreed what the problem was? – The sleep problem was clear to see, but what Michelle hadn't realized was that the sleep deprivation was causing much of the boys' daytime behaviour as well.

'Something has got to change... I'm just so tired.'

How committed was she to solving their problem?

Student nurse Michelle was physically and mentally exhausted. Her determination to solve the problem showed her to be a highly courageous and self-disciplined mum.

Was she willing to change her own behaviour?

Michelle got to grips with her need to change from the moment it was pointed out that she was not being assertive enough with her boys. (See page 38 for guidelines on how to express yourself more assertively.)

The result

Single mum Michelle was in great need of the community support that the House offered to help her reach a resolution in her boys' behaviour problems. She had a very challenging time, but over the course of the five days she helped her boys learn to settle themselves to sleep unaided, and to stay in their own beds through the night.

As a result of her in-House success she would in future be able to leave her boys with a carer or babysitter, which meant she could start to rebuild her social and support network back home.

'I've noticed a big difference in Matthew and Ross's relationship as brothers. They're a lot closer. It's just lovely seeing them that way with each other.'

Dr Tanya says...

'When you have established a new sleep routine, stick to your boundaries. Be really clear, be **really** strong. Sleep behaviour may seem to get worse before it gets better, but remember: a loving and caring parent needs to able to say "No" and follow through.'

Inside the House Toney, Alex, Tiimu (6 years 10 months) and Tobi (2)

'I have a real problem with giving up the breastfeeding, because we don't intend to have any more children.'
(Mum, Alex)

Alex and Toney Pitt arrived at the House exhausted by their son Tobi's sleep pattern. He would crawl into their bed each night and would demand constant breastfeeding. They wanted help with what they saw as Tobi's sleep problem.

What was the problem? – Tobi would settle to sleep only in his parents' bed and woke constantly through the night. Alex's partner Toney hoped she would soon stop breastfeeding.
When did the problem start? – Soon after Tobi's birth.
Why did it happen? – His mother's breast had become Tobi's main sleep cue. Suckling was the only way he could settle himself back to sleep.

Dr Tanya says...
With a child of his age you have to say no... and follow through.

Did you and your partner agree on what the problem was?

There was a difference in perception as to the extent of the problem. Toney, in his practical way, was unable initially to understand Alex's emotional response to breastfeeding. He felt she should just stop. For Alex the situation was complex and needed deep, personal consideration.

'Most of the time when he wakes up that's all I hear him saying: he wants his "boob, boob".'
(Toney)

How committed were they to solving their problem?

It was a tough challenge for the couple, but once Alex and Toney started to communicate more deeply about their involvement in the sleep problem, Alex was able to choose to stop breastfeeding.

Whose problem was it?

When on day four Tobi slept through the night in his own bed, with no protest and no need of his mother's breast, Alex realized a personal breakthrough had occurred. Tobi was ready to enjoy being a toddler and she was ready to acknowledge that he had outgrown the need for the breastfeeding relationship.

Were they willing to change their behaviour?

Alex's willingness to re-evaluate the situation made a positive difference to Tobi's development as well as her relationship with Toney.

'Really funny – first thing in the morning Tobi comes through to our room. Sometimes he'll just come in and point out that daddy's there: "Daddy look, mummy daddy", because Toney used to spend a lot of time downstairs on the sofa. Well he doesn't any more, does he?'

Breastfeeding and sleep

Many a mum has fallen into the easy pattern of letting their baby fall asleep in the parental bed while still suckling. It is convenient and it is a natural thing to do. That is why Alex (mother of Tobi) didn't think Tobi's problem related to her continuing to breastfeed. Her main concern was to stop his constant night waking. I had to explain that the continual breastfeeding was giving Tobi the message that he could only get to sleep (or get back to sleep on waking) by suckling on his mother's breast.

Of course, every mother-child relationship is different and there are plenty of mothers who continue to breastfeed their children until they are 3- or 4-years-old with no associated sleep problems. The decision to stop is always relationship-specific – but for Alex and Tobi the time was right.

Sleep associations

Children sleep well and more easily if they are surrounded by positive sleep associations – they need recognizable cues to remind them it's their habit to go to sleep in a certain way.

Sleep cues

- Appropriate sleep cues are: bathtime ➔ own bed ➔ short bedtime story ➔ bedtime kiss ➔ light out ➔ sleep.
- Inappropriate sleep cues are: falling asleep in parent's arms/ parent's body warmth/ lying in front of TV/ parental bed/ suckling on a bottle or breast ➔ sleep ➔ wake ➔ repeat.

A positive pattern becomes an accepted habit that takes place at the same time each evening. Your child will already be preparing mentally for bed from the moment they get in the bath. But, equally, children can become used to less helpful and more dependent cues.

If you let your child fall asleep on the sofa, or in your arms while you rock them, or on your breast, or on a dummy, then when they wake in the night they will not be able to get themselves back to sleep. They will have to call you back because you, and the warmth of your body, are the main associations with sleep.

Fears and imaginings

There are times when there are other reasons why your child doesn't want to go to bed. It is quite common for young children to suffer from anxiety and imaginings in the half-light of nighttime – especially in an unfamiliar situation. In the House, Harrison (5) was bothered by 'the sound of the wind' on his first night. (It was the air conditioning system!)

If your child is becoming anxious at bedtime and is starting to imagine monsters under the bed, bringing life to shadows in the closet, or thinks gremlins are causing every creak on the stairs – don't diminish your child's fears, listen to them. A child's imaginary world can seem as real as the one they inhabit with you. Try lightening their mood by helping them to change their perception:

- Zap those monsters – Take an empty plastic lemon squeezer and fill it with water. Tell your child it is a failsafe super monster-zapper and put it by their bed. Give them permission to zap if necessary (but explain that it is not to be used on their siblings, or it will be confiscated!).
- Create a friendly monster through storytelling – an older child can be encouraged to change their perception of the situation by telling a story. It might begin:
'Once upon a time there was a monster, but actually it was a really nice monster...
The idea is that the child comes to 'own' the monster. The child is in control of the situation rather than feeling anxious.

Employ the gradual withdrawal technique (see page 76) to help them to feel safe and aware of your presence as they settle and fall sleep.

If your child is whimpering or groaning in their sleep, try not to worry. This is usually just a phase. The best thing to do if it is severe is just to sit with your child; not to wake them, but to help them to settle themselves back to sleep. Little Harrison had unsettled sleep on occasion. His parents learnt to do a good job of comforting but not waking him.

It is important to realize that your child is probably not as distressed as he or she appears to be in their sleep, and although some parents choose to wake their children and then settle them back to sleep, it is not usually necessary.

If your child is very prone to fearful imaginings, take some time to get to the root cause of the anxiety. Has it been triggered by a practical event such as watching a violent

programme on TV, or being threatened by someone in the school playground?

Help your child to learn to relax by letting off steam through vigorous play early in the evening. The earlier in the evening this happens, the better it will be. A physically exhausted child will get ready for bed and be ready to drop off to sleep more easily.

However, don't make the common mistake of encouraging your kids to jump about and run around the living room an hour or less before bedtime. This will over-stimulate them and you will have much more trouble getting them to settle.

Knowing where you are (in the process)

Managing unhealthy sleep patterns in children is very challenging because they are likely to play up when you are at your most tired and vulnerable. At these times you are therefore more likely to shout, to be impatient, or to 'give in' to the easy option of bringing your child into your bed, or putting them to sleep on the sofa, rather than face the piercing agony of continuous screaming and tantrums until they learn to settle.

It may help you to stay on track if you remember how important sleep is for healthy physical and mental development. Easy sleep patterns established at a young age will stand your child in good stead later when he or she is studying for exams, or working in a stressful job. Lack of sleep affects adults negatively too and you will become more accident-prone, more stressed, over-sensitive and less able to keep your cool if you haven't had some solid quality sleep.

Keep a sleep diary

I often recommend that on the day that you change your child's bedtime routine that you get yourself a diary or create a graph ready to plot the progress and the changes. The worse the sleep problem is, the more important this will be.

It can be impossible to believe that you are making progress if you are exhausted and had to put your child back to bed 20 times in the night. However, if your notes tell you clearly that you had to return him 25 times two days previously, then you'll have objective proof that change is happening – that the process is working and that you need to persevere to succeed.

Create a bedtime routine

Sticking to a regular bedtime routine may sound like an old-fashioned notion – but believe me, it works!

A young child who is of school-age or younger should ideally be in bed by about 7.30pm. This may feel like a deprivation for those working parents who see very little of their kids during the day, but putting your child to bed is a special time for bonding in itself. Neither you nor your child should feel they are missing out, as long as you plan quality play time at other times.

If you have several children of different ages; stagger the bedtimes. This will take the pressure off you, will make an older child value their special 'extra' time, and you will also get the older children's help in reinforcing the younger one's bedtime.

Don't be tempted to be lenient with extra minutes, though. Young children are great negotiators and they soon learn to tell the time if it means staying up later!

Dr Tanya says...

'If you find your child often wanders into your bedroom at night and you are unaware that they are there, string up some noisy bells – or something else that makes a noise – so that you are alerted and can get your little one back to bed promptly.'

Forward planning

Every stage of going to bed holds potential for fun and laughter and bedtime is a period of great intimacy between you and your child. So make sure you plan ahead and start the process early enough to take account of having enough time for:

- eating.
- playing.
- undressing.
- washing.
- brushing teeth.
- saying goodnight to others in the house (or toys or pets or goldfish!).
- having a bedtime story.
- being calm and relaxed.
- having a kiss and a cuddle before you turn out the light!

Once that light is out, say your last goodnight – and mean it!

How much sleep is enough?

Sleep requirements vary from year to year and from child to child.

A 6-month-old baby needs a total of 14½ hours sleep, including a couple of naps during the day.

By the age of 2 this has reduced to 13 hours of sleep, at least 11½ hours of which should ideally be at night – possibly with a single nap during the day. (Always include naptime in your calculations.)

From the age of 3 onwards reduce the amount of sleep by ½ hour per year until the age of 9, and cut out the naps altogether.

If you find your child is waking very early in the morning, try cutting out daytime naps.

Dr Tanya says...

'Remember – play comes after tea, but before story – otherwise you'll have a wound-up child to contend with!'

Dealing with irrational fears – yours

Many parents express to me their fears that their baby or toddler may stop breathing in the night, that they may fall ill or even die without them being aware that something is wrong. Their rational mind may tell them that these events are highly unlikely, but they find themselves checking on their child all the same.

Others are nervous about bedwetting, nappy-changing or fear the child may wake in the night and not know where they are.

These are understandable responses. The difficulty is in knowing when you are disturbing your child's sleep unnecessarily.

- If you are aware that you are an anxious parent, try not to share or show your worries to your child.
- Rather than checking over-frequently and risking disturbing your child, consider investing in a baby intercom system so you can hear the sound of their nighttime chatter and breathing.
- If your child is uncomfortable or fearful, he or she is likely to wake up and let you know.
- A wet nappy will not cause a cold or other health problems, and if a child is asleep they will not be in discomfort from it. It is not drying or cleaning your baby's bottom properly that causes problems.

If reassurance doesn't work, seek help, or ask your partner (if you have one) to take on the nighttime role until your fears have passed.

Dr Tanya says...

'If your child is sick in the night or wets or soils the bed, deal with the problem with the minimum of fuss. Keep calm, do not reinforce the waking behaviour by giving it too much attention.

Gradual withdrawal

Gradual withdrawal is a very effective technique for getting children to settle themselves to sleep calmly while in your presence. It is especially useful for older children who are unused to their own bed, for children who may be used to your physical closeness as a sleep cue, or for those who are anxious due to being in an unfamiliar routine or place.

Michelle Wright used the technique to great effect in the House to help her boys Matthew and Ross learn to settle themselves to sleep.

- Every night after your child has been tucked up in bed, say goodnight but stay in his or her presence.
- Being there is not an active involvement. It's not about playtime or funny conversations, it is just about you being there to provide a comforting presence.
- Be very boring. Look away from your child and don't make eye contact.
- As the days continue, gradually move or sit further and further away from your child – until you are able to move away from the bed and out of the room altogether.
- Above all, avoid full-on cuddle contact and just sit by them and be quiet.

If he or she is obviously quite frightened or unsettled by a new experience and doesn't quite understand it – be patient. There may be quite a lot for your child to unlearn as well as newly learn.

Rapid return

Rapid return is a 'tough love' behavioural technique which works well in the case of chronic sleep problems. (Especially when combined with negative behaviour such as kicking, biting, arguing and tantrums.)

It is the nighttime equivalent to time out and requires you as the adult in the relationship to be very strong and clear about what is going on. As various parents in the House discovered, especially our stalwart Michelle, this technique takes pure grit and determination in the early stages – but it really is worth it.

Michelle started out using gradual withdrawal, but moved on to using rapid

return once the boys understood what the new sleep routine was all about.

- Settle your child in their bed, turn out the bedroom light, say goodnight and leave the room.
- If they get out of bed, which they probably will, take them back gently and straight away without getting cross and without speaking.
- Repeat this process promptly and assertively as necessary until your child falls asleep. Repeat as often as necessary.

In the case of chronic sleeping problems, you may need to keep this up throughout the night. It will be exhausting to begin with, so share the load with your partner (if you have one), and swap around the 'shifts' – making sure that you are in complete agreement about approach. It's a family matter and all of you will benefit in the long run!

Incentives, praise and reward

Whichever technique you decide to use, some bargaining may be needed in the early stages.

- Don't be too proud to negotiate a deal that promises a treat tomorrow in exchange for good behaviour today – but it shouldn't become a habit.
- If your child has been good and met the goal you have set for them – e.g. has slept through the night, or has stayed in their own bed – be liberal with praise. Then set new goals and involve them in a sense of their own achievement.
- Use a sticker chart (see page 112) so that your child can see how well they're doing.
- If your child is able to understand the concept, introduce the character of 'The Nighttime Fairy' to your child's bedtime. Explain that this fairy will be waiting to see how well they go to sleep – and when they do the fairy will add a sticker to the sleep sticker chart.
- For a reward that builds over time, with progress, place a piece of jigsaw on the pillow or next to the child's bed each night. In the morning they can add the piece to their ever-growing bedtime puzzle.

Remember: It is your behaviour which influences your child's actions. The good news is that you can influence change for the better just as effectively as change for the worse.

Dr Tanya says...

'When you adopt a behavioural approach with children, you may find that for the first night and the second night everything goes really well, but then things get bad again. The key is to be consistent; because if you are consistent whatever approach you use will work.'

One of the House dads, Alan, summed up the positive impact of an evening routine brilliantly:

'This sleeping thing just works a treat. Every night she knows the routine. Even in the bath last night Ellie just said, "Oh bathtime, storytime, bedtime." It is in there, she knows that that is what happens.'

Prior to using gradual withdrawal, his toddler Ellie was ruling the roost and had slept in their bed each and every night since the day she was born.

What I found endlessly interesting, as behaviour improved in the House, was that as parents' expectations of behaviour became more developmentally grown up, so they stopped treating their toddlers like babies. If you show clearly that you expect your child to go to bed, she goes to bed. You are treating her as an older child – and she likes that.

Dr Tanya's peaceful sleep programm

Preparation

- Make your child's bedroom a special place to be so that they look forward to being 'in their own space'.
- Shop or create with your child new sleep cues for the bedroom, such as coloured mobiles, a fluffy toy, or bedtime storybooks.
- If your child is unused to sleeping in their own bed, take time to 'introduce' them to their bed.
- Get a diary, notebook or create a graph, so you can monitor progress day to day.

Create a bedtime routine

- Choose a bedtime that is appropriate for your child's age and stage and stick to it.
- Be realistic in your aims. Don't expect radical change overnight.
- Plan your time so that your child has eaten, is washed or bathed, has changed into their sleep clothes and has had a story in time for the set bedtime.
- Keep to the same routine, even if you are away from home. If necessary, take the children's pyjamas and wash things with you. They may well enjoy the excitement of getting ready for bed away from home, and be amused at wearing 'PJs' under an outdoor coat!
- Be aware of how much sleep your child needs per night – and don't forget to take into account naptime.

Gradual withdrawal

- Every night, after you have settled your child in his or her bed, turn the light out but stay in his or her presence.
- Avoid cuddling. Just sit down and be quiet.
- Being there is not about active involvement, it is just about providing a presence.
- Be very boring. Look away from your child and don't make eye contact.
- Don't be drawn into chat or contact.
- If he or she is frightened or unsettled by an experience, be patient. There may be quite a lot for your child to unlearn as well as learn.
- As your child becomes used to the new routine,

sit further and further away from the bed.

- Don't be tempted to talk or play. Just say, 'shhh, shhh,' or keep quiet.
- Once your child is able to settle themselves to sleep quite easily, use rapid return if they wake up and get out of bed.

Rapid return

- Once you've settled your child and turned out the bedroom light, leave the room.
- If they get out of bed, take them back straight away without getting cross and without speaking.
- Say 'shhh, shhh,' gently, and then leave.
- Wait outside the bedroom door.
- If the child gets up and leaves the room, swiftly pick them up and return them to bed, with no fuss.
- With chronic sleeping problems you may need to keep repeating this through the night. It will be exhausting to begin with – but it's well worth the outcome!
- If your child is finding it hard to settle and cries or is a bit distressed, do not go back straight away but leave your child for a short period of time – between 1–5 minutes, or as long as you can bear to.
- Repeat this process as necessary until your child falls asleep.

Incentives, praise and reward

- Involve your child in their progress by making sure they understand their goals.
- Give them incentives by letting them know that they will be rewarded for their success.
- If they are old enough, show them the progress they have made on your graph.
- The reward may take the form of a sticker on the sticker chart, a favourite walk or some other treat favoured by your child.
- Try using incentives such as the jigsaw surprise or the nighttime sticker fairy (see page 77) to encourage your child to go to sleep more quickly.
- Praise them for good behaviour and do not reward the bad. In time they will understand which gets the better response from you.
- Monitor progress so that you know how far *you* have come – and give yourself *your* just reward.

4

Understanding Eating Problems and Phobias

Many parents are very anxious around the issues of food and eating. Feeding is synonymous with nurturing and survival: it is at the primitive core of parenting. So it's understandable that if a child refuses to eat, or throws a tantrum rather than try a new food, a parent will give in or compromise to get them to eat.

Eating is part of social learning. Children learn about food and eating from you and your attitude towards it. Family meals are an ideal time for being together and communicating, so try to have at least one meal together a day and encourage your child to help you prepare the food for it too.

A child can 'go off' their food for all sorts of reasons. A problem does not have to be extreme for a parent to feel frightened and despairing that their child isn't eating properly – whether that means not eating enough, not eating healthy foods, or not feeding him or her self.

For a quiet life, parents give in to their child's demands. They also give in in the hope that their child will at least eat something. Every parent wants their child to eat healthily and to have the best possible start in life. Is it any wonder that many parents have issues of anxiety relating to food and eating?

'He's just got no interest in food at all... You worry, you panic – you know? You think, "he's got to eat, he's got to eat", so you sit there and feed him.' (Paula)

'I cry quite a lot over my son. I'm so worried about him not eating that I wonder: Is he going to die?' (Nicky)

Food facts:

- Children are able to self-feed from about 10–12 months onwards (or younger if their motor skills can facilitate putting food in their mouths with their fingers or a spoon).
- Young children should not be given control over their choice of foods or their diet because their taste palette, or range of tastes, is not yet fully developed.
- Toddlers are often neophobic – they are instinctively frightened of anything new or unfamiliar. This includes anxiety about new flavours and textures.
- Resist the temptation to compromise or give in to your child's favourite food requests – they will inevitably limit themselves to safe and familiar tastes and textures. (See the friendly food programme on pages 98–9.)
- A child's stomach is smaller than an adult's, so give them small, manageable portions.
- A child who has a healthy diet and will sit and eat can be given a small number of food choices as an incentive – as they have no food-related issues.

'It's just an absolute battleground. Sometimes I don't even bother – I just let him run around while we're eating.'

(Sara)

Dr Tanya says...

'Small children can be neophobic – toddlers in particular can be afraid of new experiences. If your child has a restricted diet, don't load up their plate with stuff they don't know. Put on the plate the foods that are familiar, and only small portions of the foods that are new. Expect that up to 15–20 times they will reject it. You are putting them through a process of desensitization.'

Inside the House Steve, Paula, Jacob (4 years) and Isaac (2 years 6 months)

What was the problem? – When he was 9 months old Isaac loved his solid food, but his habits changed and he had developed an aversion to anything solid or lumpy. Older brother Jacob had no interest in food and would only eat if mum Paula fed him, so she was feeding both boys by hand. Isaac was now a worrying priority and Steve and Paula were desperate for help.

When did the problem start? – It started when Isaac was still a baby.

Why did it happen? – Steve and Paula had no idea why the problem started. The doctors had decided there was nothing wrong physiologically, so the clue had to lie in the parental history. Paula had grown-up children who had suffered no eating problems.

What had you tried in the past? The parents' concern had led them to consult medical specialists who had advised there was nothing physically wrong with Isaac.

Whose problem was it?

Paula had issues of unresolved grief relating to a period of post-natal depression soon after Isaac was born. She wanted to compensate emotionally for the time she had lost with her boys, and her sadness associated with this time impacted on the way she fed them. Totally unconsciously, she was feeding them as if they were still babies.

Once Paula and Steve recognized the problems, they worked hard together to process the past and move on in order to change their behaviour around mealtimes.

What did they do to keep the problem going?

Paula's anxiety around food had led to it dominating their lives. Her whole day was spent preparing meals for the boys and puréeing food for Isaac. Her tendency to be overly anxious about mess and food had transferred itself to Isaac and Jacob, who were not at all at ease with unfamiliar textures and tastes. Paula and Steve also used ritualized play to distract Isaac from his food in order to get something into his mouth, so he wasn't learning about food, texture or eating.

How committed were they to solving the problem?

There was a lot of love and mutual support in the family. Steve was determined to be there for Paula while she came to terms with her past, and both parents committed to following a new set of eating guidelines. A personal breakthrough occurred when Paula decided, unprompted, that it was time that Isaac's high chair was replaced by a booster chair. He was able to be a toddler at last.

Were they willing to change their behaviour?

The parents' willingness to change their approach contributed enormously to the progress they made while in the House. There were several breakthrough moments. Jacob began to feed himself for the first time when both parents were absent from the table and he

was sitting with other children who were self-feeding. Isaac started to relax around food when we introduced 'messy play' at a family picnic and he did well at a 'food Olympics' which encouraged both boys to try new foods. Isaac's first bite came in a restaurant when he tucked into a large piece of garlic bread. A heart-warming moment!

The result?

By the time the family left the House both boys were eating solid foods unaided. Paula left with greater confidence in her ability to keep up the new behaviour and determined to manage her feelings of anxiety.

'... [Isaac] will now pick up a sausage... sometimes he won't eat it but he'll pick it up... I just want to hold him so tight and say, "Well done!"' (Paula)

Inside the House Paul, Nicky and Lewis (2 years 9 months)

What was the problem? – Paul and Nicky were beside themselves with worry because their toddler, Lewis, would not eat healthy foods or anything containing lumps. He would eat roast dinners – which he loved – only if they were liquidized. He also played up unless he had toys or a story while he ate. Nicky feared that she was endangering his life because of lack of food and nutrition; and his tantrums were hard to control.

Why did it happen? – Lewis's parents were treating him as if he was still a baby: using baby language, feeding him in a high chair and still giving him a bottle. Lewis was at an age where he was beginning to understand his own power and knew how to get his parents' attention. Nicky used wet wipes constantly and acknowledged that she was obsessed with cleanliness and tidiness, which had contributed to Lewis developing a phobia surrounding anything messy.

What had they tried in the past? – Paul and Nicky were very attentive parents who fed Lewis together so that one of them could divert Lewis with books and toys while they fed him. This was turning the high chair into an inappropriate playtime.

'The thing that has surprised us most... is how quickly he has grown up since we let go of that baby stage.' (Paul)

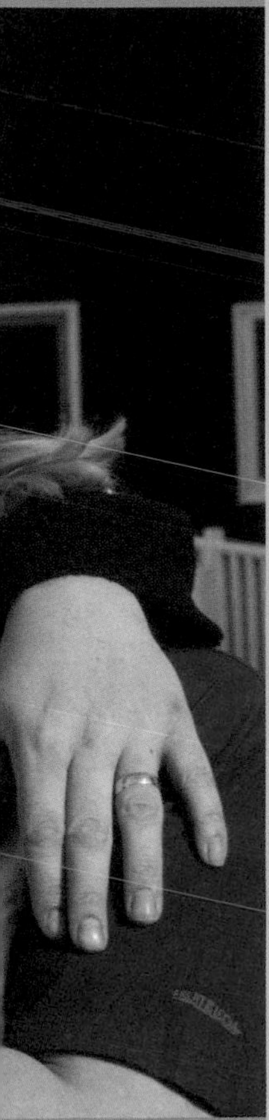

Whose problem was it?
The problem had evolved because Nicky and Paul, in their anxiety to get Lewis to eat, were too ready to give in to him rather than risk him becoming upset. As a result he ate a lot of yoghurt and other creamy foods, but no solid foods.

What did they do to keep the problem going?
Nicky's excessive concern with keeping Lewis clean by constantly using wet-wipes, and his own discomfort when his fingers became sticky, rang alarm bells. Unless Lewis became comfortable with being messy he would never learn to feed himself. During a messy picnic exercise it became obvious that Lewis was suffering from a food-related phobia.

How committed were they to solving the problem?
All Nicky and Paul wanted was their child's future well-being and happiness. There were some challenging moments for both parents as they were having trouble letting go of their baby boy and welcoming the wilful toddler stage.

Were they willing to change their behaviour?
Once Nicky and Paul recognized that they were restricting Lewis's development by over-parenting and trying to protect him from any kind of personal distress, they became ready to let go of his baby bottle and his high chair. They were also happier to encourage him to be comfortable being separate from them for periods of time.

The result?
Lewis adapted to his new-found toddler status very quickly. To his parents' delight he was soon eating handfuls of chicken and cauliflower. Nicky and Paul also adapted to becoming firmer parents and promised to banish wet-wipes forever!

Dr Tanya says…
'The more you stare intently or fuss over a child while they play with their food, the more your intensity will increase their anxiety about eating. Anxiety triggers the 'flight or fight' response: your child will either rebel (fight) against you by becoming aggressive, or will withdraw (flight) and stop eating.

Rather than fuss and exacerbate the problem, create activities that take the focus off the individual child and focus on the broader social picture. Children are very good at picking up cues.'

Inside the House Darren, Sara and Harrison (5 years 3 months)

What was the problem?
– One of the many reasons Darren and Sara brought 5-year-old Harrison to the House was for help with his eating. Harrison had never eaten a whole meal in his life. His diet consisted mainly of chocolate buttons and milk. All he would eat for lunch was a bread and butter sandwich, and sometimes he wouldn't even eat that. He had an almost obsessional need to stop different types of foods touching each other. He also had sleep problems and was rude and violent towards his parents.

When did it start?
– The problems were long-standing and dated back to Harrison's birth (see pages 28–9 for their story and how it had affected their parenting skills.)

Why did it happen?
– Sara readily admitted that she had negative feelings about Harrison and that he was most likely to hear himself talked about in a derogatory way at home. Harrison rarely saw the way a smile could transform his

'Harrison lives on bread, milk and chocolate buttons. He's never eaten a piece of fruit; never eaten a vegetable since he's been born. Trying to get Harrison to sit and eat a meal with us is an absolute nightmare.' (Sara)

Whose problem was it?

Rather than being angry and aggressive, it transpired that Harrison was feeling very sad and had received the message from an early age that he was naughty. Like Paula, Sara had issues of unresolved grief – in her case relating to a distressing story of the loss of her unborn baby daughter. When Harrison was born Sara regretted that he was not her baby girl, and the pattern of her being angry with Harrison began.

What did they do to keep the problem going?

Sara and Darren's relationship had become tense and strained and Harrison experienced a great deal of negativity. His mother's 'show home' tidiness had contributed to an eating problem that was bordering on phobic. He had sleep and behavioural problems as well.

How committed were they to solving the problem?

Once Sara and Darren witnessed the positive changes in Harrison's behaviour in the House and became aware that this little boy was acutely anxious around mess and disorder, they became determined to show him more love and affection so that he felt loved and secure. Their new approach had an immediate effect on his behaviour.

mother's face because she tended to look anxious or cross.

What had they tried in the past?
– Neither Sara nor Darren had a good word to say about Harrison in the early stages. Their key tactics were either shouting, or giving in and compromise.

Were they willing to change their behaviour?

They worked hard at changing the way they talked about and responded to Harrison and learned how much he loved his parents to be happy and smiling. Sara promised to do less housework and play more, and to continue to praise Harrison and to express her love and hug him at every opportunity.

The result?

Harrison was like a sponge – absorbing new skills and responding positively to his parents' new-found playfulness and affection. He responded very well to being rewarded using the sticker chart and his fussy eating began to disappear once his parents began praising him. The new style of attention meant he no longer misbehaved to get noticed.

The importance of routine and clear expectations

As we've looked at in other chapters (see pages 108–9), children thrive on routine and boundaries. If you have really good, clear expectations about your child's behaviour and you communicate those expectations clearly and consistently, they will become your child's expectations too.

If you make supper for the same time each night and have a 'no snacks' rule beforehand, your child's stomach will regulate itself and you will have fewer 'on demand' requests for sweets and other quick fixes.

Try to keep mealtimes as food times and encourage your child to sit in a chair, at a table. Keep your child focused on the enjoyment and taste of the food on their plate.

If you feed your child while sitting in front of the television, the whole process of eating is lost. Instead of focusing on what they are eating or the pleasure of food, the whole experience becomes just another time when they are watching telly.

It is quite common to find children wandering around the house while they are eating. Eating in those circumstances becomes 'grazing' rather than a part of a routine and structure. You will have less control over how much or what a child has eaten, and it will be harder to gauge when they are full.

Keep the food on the plate and your child at the table and instead build up your repertoire of stories and distraction methods to keep your young child's attention focused on you, and on food.

Role modelling

If a child is 'stuck' in their anxiety about food and eating, I often suggest to the parent that they sit and eat with their child. If your child doesn't know how to eat you will need to model appropriate feeding skills so that they can observe, copy and learn. But be kind and be patient – not every child will pick up the skills straight away.

- Sit with a plate of food.
- Don't sit too close to or peer anxiously at your child.
- Introduce the idea of 'finger play' and let your child use their fingers to explore the feel of the food. They are more likely to eat something they understand and are familiar with.
- Encourage your child to self-feed using their fingers.
- Over time, when he or she is ready, help them to learn to spoon-feed themselves.
- Once they are comfortable with self-feeding, introduce the idea of using a knife and fork: first show your child how to hold the

knife and how to hold the fork, then show them how to use them.

- Don't get too hung up on how properly this is done. The important thing is the eating, not the performance.
- If they find both implements a struggle, start off with the fork and introduce the knife later.
- Model appropriate feeding skills: put a small amount of food on your fork and put in your mouth with exaggerated appreciation: 'Mmmm. Yum yum. That was delicious! I think I'll have some more...'
- Smile and open your eyes wide to emphasize your enjoyment.
- Chew, swallow and pause before taking the next mouthful.
- Then encourage your little one to do the same.

Your children will learn from other children and their siblings too, so involve all your children in the learning process. It will reduce tension and become quite a game!

'He's a good boy isn't he... It won't slide back. I'm not letting it slide back. No way.'

(Darren)

Keep mealtimes fun

A young child's concentration will wander, so keep things moving. Keep mealtimes interesting and fun. Liven things up by reading stories, telling a joke, play games (but make sure you retain their positive focus on food and eating).

- Look at the plate and say: 'Aha – you've got potatoes on your plate today. Let's tell a story about Mr Potato. Mr Potato has been a very naughty vegetable. In fact, Mr Potato has been so naughty... let's put him in your mouth and chew him up!'
- Turn a plate of baked beans or a mound of mashed potato into a circus ring and bring each mouthful into the centre of the ring as an 'act' before putting it on the fork.
- Encourage your children to help you cook so that they learn to enjoy food and the process of eating.
- Cut bread into shapes and eat 'dinosaur toast' or 'fairy castle sandwiches'.

Children's learning is linked to play (see Chapter 2: The Power of Play and Praise). When children are having fun they will begin to form good new habits unconsciously – and much more easily than if parents are getting cross and saying, 'Use your knife and fork', 'Sit up straight' or, 'Stop playing with your food; eat it properly.'

If you can banish anxiety from the table and turn mealtimes into a creative and fun part of the day, they will become a time when you can enjoy being together.

Positive food associations

Lewis (2 years 9 months) was so food phobic that he would only eat dry and crispy foods; he could not bear to be near anything wet or sloppy. I decided to introduce his parents to the technique of positive food association and to use it to encourage Lewis to try mashed potato: a food he thought he disliked.

- The idea behind food association is that you introduce a small amount of the new food alongside a familiar food. In that way the flavour and texture of the new food gradually becomes familiar – and the known food acts as a treat.
- When your child eats some of the

unfamiliar food, give them some of the 'treat' food *immediately*. The idea is to reinforce the knowledge that receiving rewards is contingent upon good behaviour.

- Don't force the pace. Do a little at a time and some each day. Try not to lead, but give your child lots of encouragement and praise. If he or she doesn't want to put the food in their mouths, encourage them to touch it or smell it, so that they become familiar with what it is.

This process can lead to some bizarre food combinations: such as mashed potato and chocolate buttons, or yoghurt and roast chicken – but children don't seem to mind! In Lewis's case we had a major breakthrough as he tasted a small amount of mashed potato on day one, moved on to fruit on day two, and then a meal of chicken nuggets and chips (self-feeding) on day three. Two weeks after he returned home he was eating a full roast dinner unaided. It was an extraordinary result for this phobic little boy – and a tribute to his parents that they had remained patient and succeeded.

Messy play

One of the most effective ways of identifying food and mess phobias, and one of the most powerful ways of encouraging a child to overcome them, is via 'messy play'. (It is also a good way to test your own anxiety levels in response to mess and disorder!) Messy play is most effective if it is carried out with paint or food or papier-mâché – substances that have wet textures and a propensity to get everywhere! But such phobias can also be identified by observing the way a child becomes distressed if something is untidy, broken or disordered.

We held several messy food picnics in the House. The objective was to help anxious children such as Harrison, Lewis and Isaac to get comfortable with food. At a messy food picnic – anything goes. Encourage your child to stick a finger in a yoghurt instead of using a spoon, put jelly on dad's nose, lick a creme egg while eating a ham sandwich, or put mayonnaise on a strawberry. It really doesn't matter – the important thing is to encourage your child to touch, smell and taste as many different types and textures of food as possible.

With Harrison, his obsessive need for order extended to the way he played with his toys. His cars were always lined up in neat rows and if anyone messed them up he would simply start to tidy them up again. His behaviour was going to take time to change.

If your child becomes distressed around mess, try and figure out what is causing their discomfort. Is it just that mummy or daddy is acting in a way that is unfamiliar – or is there a food phobia at work?

Variations on the messy play theme include:

- A food fight (in our case a baked bean throwing contest) – where children are allowed to throw plates of cold food at their parents. (Outside and in overalls, of course!)
- The food Olympics – explained below.

Harrison was initially very disconcerted by the mess of the baked bean fight. He held back and announced to dad that he 'didn't like that game'. As the week went on he changed his mind, and on day six he announced that he wanted to play 'the food game'! He had assimilated the idea and was now ready to get messy. He started to eat more normally, too.

Using a sticker chart as a mealtime incentive

That wonderful device, the sticker chart (see page 112) comes into it's own at mealtimes. A few basic guidelines on a large sheet of paper can provide a great incentive for children to behave and try new foods at mealtimes.

You could encourage your child to draw up the chart with you, and put four boxes down the side to show what you'd like them to do. For example:

1 Sit nicely in your chair.
2 Use your knife and fork.
3 Behave well at the table.
4 Eat all that you are asked to eat.

Of course, the goals can relate to anything that suits your own situation. If your child gets all four stickers they can then choose their pudding; choose a game to play with you after supper; or anything else you feel is appropriate.

This isn't about adopting a strict style of parenting that insists children should be well-behaved, miniature adults who keep quiet and do as they are told at all times. This is about establishing a routine and boundaries that shape your child's behaviour in a helpful and nurturing way. The important thing is that the process should be lighthearted. It's about making food and mealtimes fun.

How to host a 'food Olympics'

We hosted a 'food Olympics' in the House to build on Jacob's new-found enthusiasm for self-feeding, but more particularly to encourage Isaac to try solid foods in a playful environment where he was put in gentle competition with his older brother. It was so successful that we repeated the activity on the last day to reinforce Paula's confidence in herself as a parent who could bring about change in her children.

The set up:

- Line up five plates in a row for each child.
- On each plate put a foodstuff of different taste and texture. Start with a familiar food, build up to the more challenging ones and end with the positive reinforcement of a sweet or easy-to-eat food.
- We used: biscuits, crisps, a slice of pizza, raw carrot and chocolate yoghurt.
- Cover each plate with a bowl. We used brightly-coloured plastic ones.
- At the end of the course put a prize. Keep it visible so that the child has an incentive to keep going.

And they're off!

- The objective is to start at plate one and to finish at plate five, and to have sampled (or touched) each of the foods.
- Every time the child lifts the lid to reveal the food and takes a bite – or eats the whole plateful – they have won the right to move on to the next dish.
- Give them enthusiastic encouragement.
- Ignore unwanted behaviour and focus on the good behaviour.
- Encourage a more anxious child to learn from others around the table.
- Avoid over-praising the child with the problem at the expense of praising a better behaved, role-model sibling.
- If a child is very negative about a particular food, act as a role model and demonstrate how to eat the food, encouraging them to do the same. If it is all too much for them, suggest that they simply touch or lick the food and then move on.

Before you begin you need to be prepared not to reward a child who does not finish the course, otherwise you undermine the learning point of the activity.

Strike a balance

- The key to effective praise is to remain relaxed and calm. Don't hover. Be sincere, but not hysterical. If you over-praise and over-stimulate the child with excessive enthusiasm they will lose track of what it is you are rewarding and will feel overwhelmed.
- Sometimes it is important to let your child find their own way through the problem. Consider putting a mirror in a prominent position so that you can watch unobtrusively without 'cramping their style'.

Curbing anxiety – yours

At the root of almost every child's eating problem that I have experienced is an anxious parent; and often an anxious parent who is also obsessively clean and tidy.

If you fear you are transmitting your behaviour to your child:

- Keep your behaviour calm and consistent. Have fun with food.
- Don't pile your child's plate high with food – it will increase their anxiety levels, and yours. Generally speaking, a child's stomach is about the same size as their fist. You could use that as a guideline.
- Resist the temptation to wipe your child's mouth a lot. Just imagine if, the next time you and your partner were going out for a nice meal, your partner frequently and randomly ran a heavily-scented wet-wipe across your face. It might just put you off your food and ruin the evening!
- Watch your language. If you know you get frustrated around mealtimes, make a conscious decision to smile and banish the word 'don't' from your vocabulary.
- If your child keeps saying, 'I don't want this, I don't want that'; take time to assess whether they are food phobic or just being fussy. A neophobic child will take several attempts before they become desensitized enough to be able to touch or try an unfamiliar food. A fussy child, on the other hand, needs to know that there will be consequences if they do not eat even a little of the food.
- Rather than fuss over your child and risk exacerbating an eating problem, divert your attention elsewhere.
- If your concerns lie more with keeping the place tidy and having a child who knows how to hold their knife and fork correctly, then please review your priorities. Your child may not be ready for that developmental step just yet.
- If you're looking for an objective picture, why not ask a friend or your partner to video you with your child at mealtimes? Ask for some honest feedback from them and see what patterns you can observe when you play the video back.

Success is about laying the foundations of really good, clear expectations of the kinds of behaviour that are okay at mealtimes. Use all your creative parenting tools to make mealtimes fun, but be realistic about your child's behaviour – whether it is defiant or phobic – and manage your anxiety accordingly.

Dr Tanya's friendly food programme

Food do's and don'ts

- Don't give your child full control over food choices and diet; they do not have the knowledge and experience to make nutritious choices.
- If you give in to your child's requests for favourite foods before, or instead of, meals they will have less desire to eat at mealtimes or to try new foods.
- A child's stomach is smaller than an adult's, so give them small, manageable portions.
- You can give your child full control over self-feeding from about 10–12 months (or earlier), by introducing them to finger-feeding themselves.

Faddy eating

- Be aware that toddlers and young children are instinctively frightened of anything new or unfamiliar.
- Don't introduce a lot of new foods or textures at once. Introduce them slowly, one at a time.
- If your child picks up a piece of hated food, such as broccoli, licks it and puts it down again, resist saying, 'Don't play with your food; eat it or leave it,' or, 'Put it in your mouth and chew it.'
- Do say, 'Well done, good girl, I'm really proud of you.' But don't over-praise, as it will diminish the impact of the words.
- If your child normally eats quite happily and plays up only occasionally at mealtimes, you are probably facing a tantrum rather than an eating problem. Turn to Chapter 5 for guidance on behavioural techniques.
- Keep a food diary.
If your child is otherwise well behaved, and seems unduly distressed only at mealtimes, start to make a note of what triggers the behaviour: whether it is particular types or textures of food, whether it is related to food temperature, food quantity, or to your own mood or anxiety at mealtimes.
- Some eating problems can be very entrenched. If you're finding it hard to cope, speak to your GP or other health professional for advice.

Over-parenting

- If both parents are involved in the feeding process, change your pattern and take turns: do one meal at a time. It can be overwhelming for a child to have to please both parents as well as getting to know new foods.
- Try not to peer at your child – full of anxiety – while they eat, or tell them what to do in a bullish way. Instead, praise them sincerely when they do something well, and keep your tone light and non-judgemental.
- Be aware when the time is right to let go of the paraphernalia of babyhood. Say goodbye to the bottle, high chair and helping with feeding, and say hello to booster seats, cutlery and self-feeding.

Positive parenting skills

- Be a role model for your child and show them how to eat and behave well.
- Set up a routine for meals and eating. Explain what is expected – and stick to it.
- Be enthusiastic about food

and encourage a readiness to try new foods.

- Use non-verbal expression to show your enthusiasm and smile!
- Encourage and praise at every opportunity, but don't overdo it.
- Focus on and praise the child who is doing well, more than the one who is seeking attention by behaving badly.
- Stage your praise. Reward periodically and increase the time between rewards. Partial reinforcement is more powerful then constant and total reinforcement.
- See Chapter 5 on behaviour for clear guidelines on praising and rewarding children.

Make mealtimes fun and a time for bonding

- Make up stories relating to the foods on the plate.
- Turn your fork into an aeroplane that flies in a circle before it lands in your child's mouth.
- Make a face out of the food on your child's plate.
- Use incentives such as stickers to help mark your child's progress at mealtimes.
- Encourage your child to take a spoonful of food every time you close your eyes.
- Encourage your child to be involved in preparing food; it will help them to gain positive associations with food.
- Mealtimes are a great opportunity to spend time together as a family.
- Make mealtimes a social occasion. Enjoyment of food is not solely about eating.

Introduce messy play

- Children who may be phobic will benefit from having contact with different kinds and textures of food.
- Use games such as the food Olympics (pages 95–6) or a food fight (page 94) to understand more about your child's anxiety levels around food and mess.
- Enjoy a weekly indoor picnic to reconnect your child to food.
- Buy pasta with your child in the supermarket. Get them to hold it and to make a picture with it. Then cook pasta for supper and show them the difference in texture between the cooked and raw pasta.

Reduce your own anxiety levels

- Keep your behaviour calm and consistent. Have fun with food.
- Resist the temptation to use wet-wipes during a meal – it is not a pleasant experience for your child.
- Praise your child for trying a mouthful of an unfamiliar food in a calm way, or your child will be bewildered.
- Children are very good at picking up cues. If there are other children eating nearby, use one of them as a role model.
- If your concerns are more to do with keeping the home tidy and having a child who knows how to hold their knife and fork correctly, then you need to review your priorities.
- If you feel you can't do it on your own, then please seek help. (See Further Resources page 156.)

5 Taming Uncontrollable Behaviour

In order to survive socially and to develop friendships, your child will benefit from developing social skills: being able to listen to others, to share, care, and learn to communicate in a positive manner. Their behaviour toolbox will need to include: manners, respect, and the ability to learn some self-control.

The challenge for parents is to put behaviour guidelines in place from an early age that will shape the behaviour of their child in a constructive way – but without crushing their spirit.

'I want my child to do as I ask,' you may be thinking, 'but I'd hate him or her to become totally compliant'. And you would be right. Good behaviour does not mean creating good, sweet children who conform to a romantic (and rather unrealistic) ideal; it is about them learning 'appropriate' behaviours and how to be assertive while treating others with respect. In our modern world a child needs positive self-esteem and the ability to let their character shine through. They need to be resourceful and resilient and to know who they are. There is no harm in healthy rebellion and a show of individuality on occasion.

There will be times in your child's life when good behaviour will mean having the ability to say 'no' rather than 'yes', and having the confidence to walk away from a situation they feel uncomfortable in. Having the courage of their convictions is an equally important part of the behavioural development.

What's the problem? Understanding your child's behaviour

When your child is making unreasonable demands, what do they really want? The simple answer is: your attention. But is he or she in distress or simply play-acting in order to get what they want? What lies behind their behaviour, and how on earth can you change it? This chapter takes a brief look at child development and explains how to use the practical, long-established behavioural techniques that we used with great success inside the House of Tiny Tearaways.

What is the difference between personality and character?

'Your personality is who you are. Your child was born with a personality that is theirs alone, born of the unique genetic mix of his or her parents. Your character is more malleable: it develops through what you learn and shows in the way that you project yourself. Your child's character develops over time in response to environmental influences at home, at school and in society.'

Your child's brain: frontal lobe development

You may wonder why it is so difficult to get young children to learn the difference between right and wrong – there is a logical explanation.

A lot of the problems that we have as parents stem from our expectation that our children have an understanding of the motives behind their behaviour. But in the early years, they don't. This is because the parts of the brain that deal with social behaviour and moral understanding – the frontal lobes – do not develop fully until about the age of three.

The frontal lobes are at the front of the brain, protected by the skull. Until they are fully developed a child has no ability to process moral argument in a meaningful or emotional way. He or she may sit there saying, 'yes, yes, yes' while you explain the unfairness of kicking, biting or snatching – but all you are doing is reinforcing the behaviour you don't want by giving it a huge amount of attention.

How we shape the behaviour of our children in the early years will impact on the development of their thinking. It is our parental responsibility to make sure we coach our children in a way that will healthily shape their social behaviours and moral understanding. In essence, with younger children, actions speak louder than words.

Development facts

- Babies have no sense of being separate from you as a parent. Their entire existence revolves around being dependent upon you for food, survival and a sense of routine.
- From the ages of approximately twelve months to two years onwards, a young child will begin to develop a sense of personal identity. They will start to test 'what is allowed' in order to understand that they are separate from you.
- This can be a particularly difficult time for parents who find it hard to believe the speed of change in character. Toddlers are like miniature teenagers, testing their new-found independence. At this age, ignoring bad behaviour and rewarding good behaviour is the most effective response.
- Once your child is at school full time and learning to be separate from you, it is possible to have a basic conversation about their behaviour and its consequences.

There are two simple principles at the foundation of everything I taught parents in the House. They are:

- Ignore bad behaviour.
- Reward good behaviour.

It really is that simple.

Ignore bad behaviour

The natural reaction – and the most common mistake – when you want to stop your children from doing something naughty, is to tackle the situation by confronting them head on, or telling them off about it. The reason this approach is flawed is because you are giving your child, and the unwanted behaviour, attention. Lots of attention! Possibly more attention than you would give them if they were doing something good.

The truth is that spotlighting negative behaviour makes it happen more often. On the other hand, if you chill out and relax, your child will chill out and relax, and the problem is more likely to go away.

'Learning to be separate from parents and to develop individuality is part of being a toddler.'

Dr Tanya says...

'The message to get across to children is: if you scream, we don't pick you up, if you play nicely, we do.'

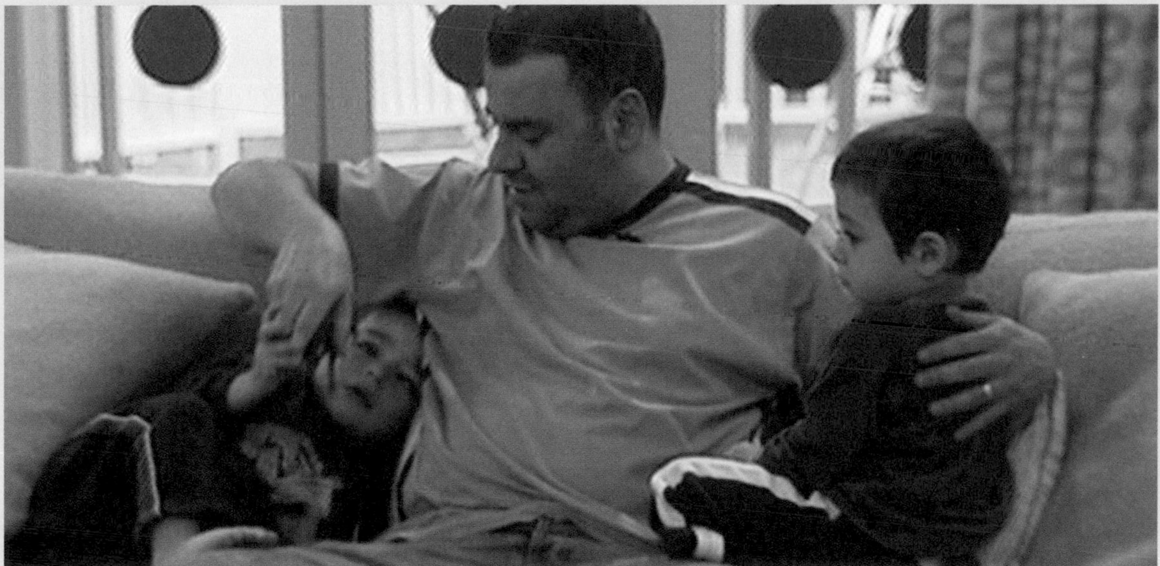

Bulent, father to twins Konur and Emir (2 years 6 months) and older son Hakan (4 years) turned into a perfect ignorer while he was in the House. Previously rather unconfident in his parenting skills, he took the 'ignore or reward' guidelines to heart. The rules I gave him were:

- When the tantrums start, make sure both boys are safe – but then ignore them.
- If Emir stops crying first, go to him and praise him for stopping.
- Bring him with you – away from Konur who may still be crying – and start to play or read with Emir.
- As soon as Konur stops crying, go to him and praise him for stopping. If he starts crying again (because he thinks you are still in your old habit of attending to upset behaviour), tell him there's no need to cry, and as soon as he stops he can come and play too. Then leave him and walk away without speaking.
- As soon as Konur learns, and stops, go to him and praise him for stopping. Bring him over to join the game.
- Give both boys lots of praise and attention.
- They are learning that when they are lovely, they have got daddy.

Bulent sat between his boys on the sofa reading a story. When one of his boys played up he turned his whole body away from the screaming child – rather like an impenetrable wall. The impact was powerful – and very effective. It boosted Bulent's confidence in himself as a parent, as well as teaching the boys how to behave.

The additional benefit of this was the additional attention that Hakan got as a result. A thoughtful and well-behaved older child, he had been missing out on praise and attention at the expense of his lively younger brothers.

Reward good behaviour

The positive flip side of ignoring bad behaviour is to reward the good. The more you comment on, praise and reward good behaviour, the more of it you will get. The positive reinforcement helps children to retrain their brain to focus on reward and motivation and the warmth of positive attention.

Cuddles, love, attention, stories and games all combine to make your child realize that it is more fun to be good than naughty. (See the creative play programme on page 59 for ideas on positive reinforcement.)

Being an upbeat and focused parent

Children, like adults, respond positively to warmth and enthusiasm and negatively to frowns or disapproval. We all like to feel we're wanted and that our nearest and dearest enjoy having us around. To encourage your child to behave well it helps if you smile at them and encourage them regularly in their activities. If being with you is an exciting and happy experience, they will be less likely to want to misbehave or get on the bad side of you and risk missing out on the fun.

Being positive is not the same as being lenient and saying 'yes' to every demand, however. That way danger and chaos lies. A responsible parent needs to teach their child boundaries and self-control.

Clarity is the key. The clearer you are in expressing your expectations of your child's behaviour – the positive rewards if they behave well, and the negative consequences if they don't – the easier your life, and theirs, will be.

Setting boundaries

Behaviour boundaries are important. They help a child to define who they are and

where they belong; they also enable a child to learn what is acceptable behaviour and what is not. This is important knowledge and self-discipline that they will transfer to other environments beyond the home.

Parents often say to me, 'Oh, I just give in for a quiet life because I know he (or she) will have a massive tantrum if I don't.' The key issue is that if a child doesn't know where they stand, they don't feel contained and they don't feel safe. If they don't feel contained and safe they will keep testing, to see what they can get away with, until they find out where the boundary actually lies. As a result, behaviour will escalate out of control. So if you don't set a clear boundary you will make the behaviour problem worse.

If you are planning to set new boundaries for a child who has never had them, you will probably get some emotional kick-back in the early stages. You will overcome this if you persist – firmly and consistently – and are strong in following through with consequences, rather than issuing empty threats. Once he or she gets used to the idea that you mean it, your child will soon learn where they stand and you will find their behaviour will settle.

Dr Tanya says

'Children who don't have boundaries feel very uncomfortable – and they will try to create their own. They will act up to get you to create a boundary. They are asking you to say no.'

The importance of routine and structure

Boundaries exist within routine and structure, and a good routine will reinforce the boundaries that you set.

If your child knows that supper time is at a certain time and that he or she will be expected to sit at the table, in a chair, and behave well (and that they will be rewarded if they manage this), then they will readily accept that this is going to happen each day, and your life will be much easier. For the routine to work, the child also needs to understand the consequences of not behaving well when expected to, and you need to be prepared to follow through if they play up. An empty threat will undermine all your good intentions. (See Consequences on page 111.)

Likewise, a good bedtime routine will reinforce the boundaries you set around bedtime and the expectations that you have of their sleep behaviour. Provided you are consistent and firm in your intentions, your child will start to self-regulate their own behaviour as you overcome old learnt patterns and the routine gradually becomes entrenched as a new, good habit.

How to set a boundary

Setting a boundary is simple: decide what behaviour you want – whether that means not fighting at the lunch table, not having a tantrum at bedtime, not hitting, swearing, biting, and so on.

- Tell your child clearly, simply and firmly that you don't want that behaviour. (There is no need to enter into a long explanation or a moral debate.)
- Explain that if they continue with that behaviour there will be a consequence.
- Explain what that consequence is (e.g. their favourite toy will be banished to the top shelf, they will forfeit going shopping/watching TV this afternoon).
- Prepare to tell them, 'Once nicely, once firmly'. (See page 110.)
- Be prepared to follow through.

Dr Tanya says

'It's about having boundaries, but being flexible enough in your approach to allow some healthy rebellion on occasion.'

Julie had a lot of trouble getting Ellie (2) to do as she was asked. She and I practised a role-play to help her find a way to put her daughter's shoes on, and I directed her through the process:

- Say, 'I'd like you to put your shoes on.'
- Go down to her level, look her in the eye and say, 'Put your shoes on, now!'

If she doesn't, you can:

- Choose to turn it into a game of 'Don't do it (Do it!)' (page 54): 'I bet I can't put your shoes on before you can...' 'I bet we can't do it before you count to 20...'
- Use distraction: 'Oh my goodness – what's that that just went past the window?' Then, while she is looking, put her shoes on.
- Threaten a consequence: 'If you don't put your shoes on I'm going to take your favourite doll and put it on that top shelf.'
- Follow through and do it.
- Ignore bad behaviour.

If there is a massive tantrum or aggression: ignore it.

- Use time-out (see pages 116–17).
- If the behaviour continues and she doesn't respond to your other, more calm approaches, put her in her room to cool down.

'I pick her up when she is having a tantrum because she is getting too upset – and I don't like her being upset.'

Parents can develop a fear of their child's reaction and become anxious at the thought of a tantrum or having a battle of wills. Pause for a moment and remind yourself who the adult is in the relationship and then say assertively, without shouting: 'Just put your shoe on!' ... 'Just DO it!'

Remember: if your child was about to run out under a truck, you would find the voice to bring them to a halt. Think about everyday discipline as a rehearsal for a time when you need him or her to respond to you quickly and unquestioningly.

Ask once nicely, ask once firmly

If you've ever had to resort to screaming at your children because they won't do as they're told, you will already know that screaming loses its impact over time and doesn't work. The more parents scream the more children become desensitized (or traumatized) and will either withdraw emotionally or play up more.

If you want your child to do something you need only ask them twice. Ask them once, nicely, and then ask them once, *firmly*. Explain the consequences of not doing what they are asked – and be prepared to follow through if they do not.

Parental assertiveness comes in handy here. You need to learn to use your facial expressions and body language effectively, and to say, 'No' as if you mean it. (See page 121.)

Your tone of voice or a particular look on your face, will teach your child that you are serious about the consequences if they misbehave; and they will learn to think, 'I'd better not push her.'

In the early stages of teaching new behaviour life may not be that simple. So you may need to combine the 'once, twice' approach with time out for your child. (See page 117.)

As already mentioned, a child under three is unable to make moral decisions about the right or wrong of a situation. However, by the time your child has turned four or five and is at school, he or she will be spending a lot of time away from you, learning to exist in a world where other children will have experiences different from their own. They will start to ask 'why?' as they test the boundaries you have set.

It is possible to have a conversation with your child about their behaviour by this age, but you still need to keep clear boundaries

in place, with clear understanding that they will be told once nicely, once firmly; and if they don't do as they are asked there will be a consequence. Explanations about the morality of behaviour and personal accountability aren't appropriate until your child reaches three upwards (depending on the child), when they will begin to understand that, 'You may want to do x, but you can't if doing x is unfair to everyone else.'

Consequences

Following through is often what parents find the most difficult. They make empty threats the whole time for all sorts of reasons (tiredness, laziness, dread of a tantrum, low confidence as a parent, fear of their child crying or of their emotional rejection.) Remember that every time you don't follow through with a consequence you are making a nonsense of the boundary you have set and undermining your previous progress. It will also be harder to stand firm tomorrow. If there are two of you involved you need to take a joint stand and help your partner to stay strong when the going gets tough.

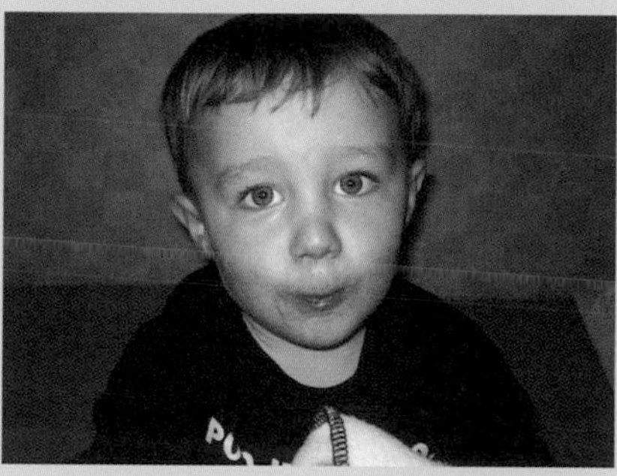

Ryan (2 years 6 months) was a wilful toddler. He would use everything in sight as a missile: apples, bananas, books, ornaments...! What was interesting to me, when watching the family profile, was that there was no real consequence for him playing up. Fiona and Mark were not assertive with him as parents and had a general philosophy that kids should be happy for as much of the time as possible. They didn't want Ryan to be upset; not realizing that Ryan was reading the situation as, 'Well, it's fine, I'll just do it again, then'.

Unified and consistent parenting

A united or consistent approach to parenting is crucial to the success of shaping behaviour in your child. If you find it hard to agree on an approach, remind yourselves: if you can't set a boundary and follow through now, what are you going to do later in life? It is much more difficult to manage a teenager.

Boundaries and following through are about developing self-awareness in your child, and also about developing your child's respect for the fact that you have a point of no return. If you and your partner have a split parenting style, or parent separately, please revisit Chapter 1 and consider drawing up a parenting contract. Your young person needs you to care about them enough to put aside any differences and take a shared approach.

Sticker charts

A parent's secret weapon; the power of the sticker as a simple and effective reward for good behaviour is remarkable. You will find that the true value of a pack of stickers far outweighs what you paid for them! A sticker chart is a deceptively simple and highly effective tool for reminding your little one of your wishes and expectations of their behaviour, as well as your intentions. It also reminds you of the importance of regularly reinforcing behaviour in a positive way. (The functions of a sticker chart are shown on the chart opposite.)

Guidelines for using sticker charts

Sticker charts work because they are driven by incentive and rewards, and the child can see for themselves that they are getting better at something. They also have visual proof of praise and recognition for their efforts. A chart gives both parent and child a sense of satisfaction as it provides a clear picture of progress and success.

A chart also allows you to identify the 'hot spots' of the day and to focus in on a difficult time – for example, getting ready for school. Divide half an hour into 5-minute slots, so that you attend and reward rapidly over that period and the child's learning is intensified. Once that period is on track you can expand the timeframe upwards to 10 minutes every hour, to every 15 minutes during the morning, to once every half hour during the day, and so on. Be flexible: design a chart that suits your particular needs.

Charts can be drawn up in a matter of moments and do not have to be sophisticated works of art – although it helps if they are child-friendly and colourful in style. Involve your child in designing and decorating their sticker charts so they have a sense of ownership. The process is done *with* them, not *to* them.

A sticker chart shows:

A goal
- What you want your child to do.
- How you want your child to behave.

A timeframe
- How long you want them to behave for.

The period of time needs to be clear, reasonably short, and fixed in length: for an hour, the length of a car journey, while at the dentist, etc. Split the time into equal slots of 5 (or 10, or 15) minutes, and at the end of every 5 minutes reward your child with a sticker.

A reward
- There is a gain for them at the end of the timeframe.

This is a promise and must be kept to if the sticker chart is to work as an effective tool. For example, 'If you are a good girl in the car today you can have your friend Jessica round when we get home.' (Rewards need to be as immediate as possible. Tomorrow is too far away to a small child.)

Incentives
- Mini rewards are given in the form of stickers to show they are progressing towards their goal and main reward.

Plenty of praise and cuddles if they manage themselves well.

Consequences
- Negative progress warnings – in the form of unhappy faces. (For example, if a child has a tantrum and does not respond to your warnings or discipline.)

One unhappy face can be overturned by having a reward sticker stuck on top of it, if behaviour improves within the time slot. (Children are allowed to be naughty at times!) Two unhappy faces together cannot be overturned. This means there has been significant poor behaviour with no attempt to apologize or be good. Your child will be ignored for poor behaviour. If there are more unhappy faces than stickers, you may decide your child should forfeit their reward.

Review
- At the end of the timeframe, review the chart with your child and cross through the double faces so that he or she is connecting with what they are learning. Explain why they are, or are not, having their treat. It is only human to misbehave sometimes, though, so don't expect perfection. One set of two unhappy faces is allowed.

Progression
- Proof of progress clearly over a set timeframe.

Success
- Improvement (or lack of improvement) in clear, visual form. With your help they will learn from the experience.

You will be able to see a clear pattern of behaviour and will be able to assess what the causes and triggers of naughtiness might be.

A getting up chart

A getting up chart can be a useful way of teaching your child to control their behaviour and learn new skills, while containing a wilful child's behaviour so that the rest of the family can prepare for their day without stress. If the situation allows, you could add everyone's name to the chart to encourage social learning.

- Draw a rectangle on a sheet of paper and divide it into columns – make one column per person.
- Decide on the behaviours you are monitoring and list them down the left side of the chart. For example:

  Get up when mummy or daddy asks you.
  Get dressed nicely.
  Clean your teeth after breakfast.
  Behave nicely on the way to school.
- Draw a horizontal line across the chart under each behaviour so you have a grid of squares.
- During the morning:

  Good behaviour is rewarded by stickers.

  Bad behaviour gets an unhappy face and requires an apology or a positive response to behaviour-control.
- If your child disregards your warnings, give them a second unhappy face. This cannot be overturned with a sticker.

You need to have the courage of your convictions and to follow through with the consequences you set if the sticker chart is to be effective. (See previous page.) Sticker charts can be used in many situations and to monitor most kinds of behaviour.

An added bonus for children is that a sticker chart helps them to make sense of passing time. Time moves more slowly and has a different meaning for a child than for an adult.

Dr Tanya says...

'There is a lot of debate about smacking. I take an anti-smacking stance because there is always a more constructive way to encourage behaviour change. By smacking your child in response to something you don't want them to do, you are also sending the message that "hitting people is okay, because I do it".'

'Your young person needs you to care about them enough to put aside any differences and take a shared approach.'

Using distraction techniques

Stickers also classify as a very effective distraction technique. Distraction techniques are a great tool because they have the power to change mood and outcomes in an instant. They are also handy to help distinguish between true distress and play-acting in a child. Putting a few seconds between the child's thoughts and their out of control behaviour can be enough to stop the negative behaviour. If the crying stops and the tears stop too, you know the moment of crisis is over and you can build on the positive change in mood.

Distraction also works well in groups of children. If one child is behaving well and the other one badly, divert your attention to the 'good' child and have some fun. The child who is playing up may well calm down and follow suit. This works particularly well at mealtimes.

Sarah used distraction techniques well with Kelsey when she was having a tantrum, by saying, 'It's very quiet in here, isn't it?' 'Where have all the other children gone?' The tantrum would then pause.

Sarah was also very good at spotting imaginary spiders to get Kelsey's attention, and would divert her focus to what other children were doing to get Kelsey engaged in the bigger picture.

Role play and learning from others

Role play is not so much a method of discipline as a way of teaching a new behaviour. You could think of role-play as an advanced form of distraction technique. It is especially appropriate if your child is upset because they are anxious and unsure of what to expect. A child who does not know what to do, or is unnerved by a new experience is likely to 'kick off'. Sometimes they need reassurance by being shown what to do.

Saying, 'Let daddy show you', 'Mummy do it', or, 'shall I go first?', will demystify an activity and show that it is safe. It also has the benefit of teaching your child a new skill, such as:

Eating a new food.

Playing a new game.

Meeting a new person.

Siblings and peers can also be valuable role models for each other. Children usually know the roles even if they choose to ignore them. They are often at their most well-behaved when demonstrating to each other the 'proper' way to do something.

Time out

Time out was used frequently in the House because many parents were dealing with fairly extreme behaviour that needed to be brought under control quite quickly. Generally speaking, time out is an action of emergency or a last resort and it needs to be used wisely, because if it is over-used it will lose its impact.

It is used:

- *After* you have tried ask once nicely, and once firmly.
- *After* you have tried ignoring the behaviour.
- *After* you have tried distraction.
- *After* all these have failed to work.

It is also used:

- When your child has been violent – especially towards another child.
- When your child has lost control and can't be reasoned with.
- When your child is being anti-social by swearing, etc.
- Or, when *you* feel you are losing it. It's a good way to give yourself some space and time if things are getting too much. But it needs to be used as soon as the problem occurs – not 'when we get home', or 'later'.

What should a time out be?

Time out is an extreme form of ignoring. It is used as a period of time for the child to cool off and reflect. For one minute for each year of the child's life he or she should be given absolutely no attention. Some people like to use a step or a chair. I often recommend putting a child alone in a room. The more boring the room, with few distractions, the better.

There is also a holding form of time out that can be used in public – described on page 134.

The rules of time out:

If it is a last resort – having tried the other behaviour methods – give your child a warning so they know that time out will happen next.

If it is an emergency, skip the warning and go to the next stage.

- Say to your child, 'You are going into time out. Now!'
- Carry or take them to their room (or time out spot), put them there and close the door.
- Don't lock the door, but hold it shut and tell them you are doing so, so that they know you're there (and don't think they are locked in).
- Ignore their behaviour completely and do not talk through the door.
- Hold the door shut for one minute of each year of their lives. Time it, don't guess – and don't give in to the temptation to extend or reduce the time.
- Remember: this is an extreme form of ignoring and the child needs to feel the impact of that if it is to work. Ignore kicks, screams, shouts or the sounds of a bedroom being destroyed! You are teaching your child an important lesson.
- When the time is up, open the door and tell your child that they can come out.
- Look them in the eye and tell them briefly why they were in time out and that if the behaviour is repeated they will go back in again.
- If the tantrum is ongoing, ask your child once nicely and once firmly to stop.
- If they are unable to calm themselves down, explain that time out will be repeated if they don't stop.
- Repeat the process – for the same period of time.
- Once your child has calmed down, explain why they were put into time out. Ask for an apology and give your child a cuddle.
- Then it's over – your child has 'done their time'. Don't hark back to the event or bear a grudge. At the first opportunity after the event, give your child lots of praise and cuddles. This reinforces the message and helps them to distinguish between 'right' and 'wrong' behaviour.

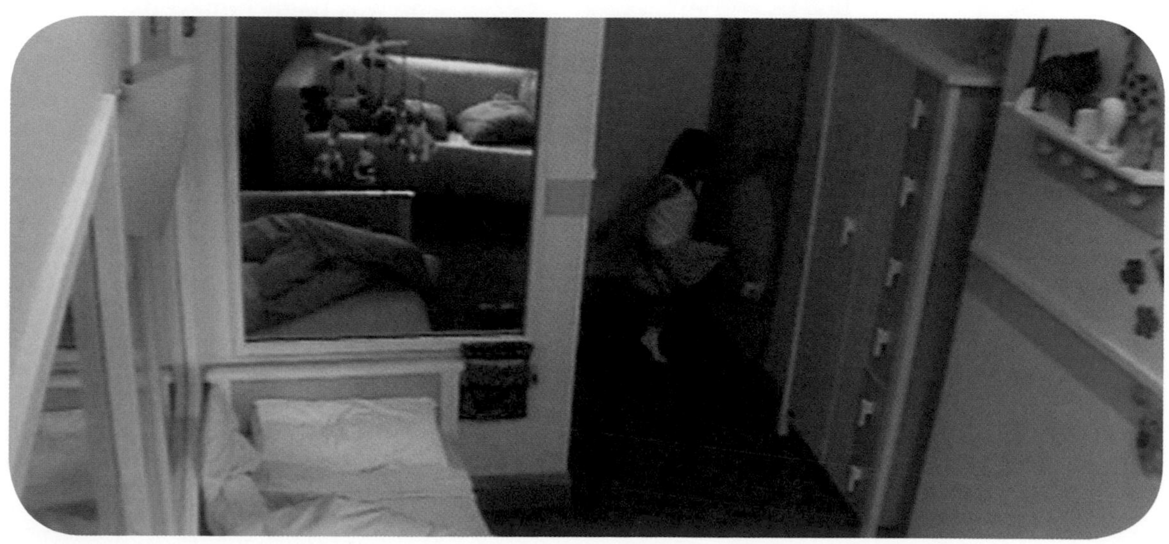

Inside the House Anita and Jaden (3 years)

'The tantrums are generally quite like a little volcano erupting.'

What was the problem? – Anita's son Jaden was out of control a lot of the time and used the 'F' word constantly, which caused Anita a great deal of embarrassment.

When did the problem start? – The problem had evolved over time.

Why did it happen? – Anita was not by nature a disciplinarian and as a result her son had few behavioural boundaries. She had got into the habit of giving him too much attention when he was badly behaved.

What had she tried in the past? – Anita had frequently told him off, but had no consistent approach to managing his behaviour.

Whose problem was it?

Jaden was being treated like a surrogate partner and was definitely 'the man in charge' at home. It was getting to the point where Anita was embarrassed to go out with him because of his tantrums and language.

What did she do to keep the problem going?

Anita gave Jaden her constant attention; whether he was good or bad. She also tried to reason with him at an age when he was too young to fully understand.

How committed was she to solving the problem?

Jaden's swearing was so persistent that I decided to teach Anita time out before any of the other parents had arrived in the House. This was necessary because children pick up on each other's behaviour very fast.

Anita took time out very seriously and used it frequently while she was in the House.

Was she willing to change her behaviour?

Anita realized that she needed to be consistent and persistent in her approach to Jaden to get positive results and she was determined to change her parenting style from friend to mother.

The result

The reward for all Anita's work came on day three in the House when Jaden was filmed sitting on his mother's bed calling out for milk. About to swear, suddenly the breakthrough happened: Jaden started to talk to himself. 'Don't say that word', he said.

Using sticker charts she also began to teach him to shape his behaviour.

Another of the parents who took time out to heart was Michelle. Her boys, Matthew and Ross, were used to rough play and sometimes stepped over the mark with other children. Hitting, biting or otherwise aggressive behaviour is never acceptable and the parental response needs to be immediate. Michelle used time out and assertive behaviour to great effect in getting them to understand what was acceptable behaviour and what was not. It was clear that she had come a long way in the House when she managed her first double time out, with one boy in the bedroom and the other with her, outside the door.

Special needs

Tracey and Bulent had a particularly difficult set of challenges with their twin boys, Emir and Konur, because the boys had been diagnosed with speech and language learning difficulties. Their tantrums were loud, long and draining – enough to test the resolve of even their devoted parents. The behavioural problems were compounded by the parents – who gave these rages too much attention – and there was work to be done to improve that. But it was clear that the challenges for them and for the boys would be ongoing, and beyond the scope of a week in the House.

Special needs in children often show up first in behavioural problems. Deafness, ADHD, dyslexia and other conditions can all inhibit your child's ability to interpret and understand the world. If you suspect your child has specific difficulties, get your GP on board and seek the advice of specialist professionals.

Importantly, if you have more than one child, try to ensure that you do not neglect the needs of your more well-behaved child. Praising good behaviour and ignoring bad behaviour remains a healthy principle – no matter what the disability.

The importance of saying 'sorry' and forgiveness

If children don't cry, if children don't rage and then learn to manage tears and rage with our help, then they will never learn how to deal with it and they will become angry adults.

Learning to say sorry and being able to forgive are a part of the process of learning about appropriate behaviour. To say sorry is to acknowledge that you understand you have stepped outside a boundary and caused other people distress. But the word has to be said with feeling, and mean something – that's why you don't ask for the 'sorry' until after you have delivered the consequence.

Forgiveness is an acknowledgement of understanding and drawing a line under the past. It has a way of making people feel good, too. Forgiving your child gives you the chance to reassure them that you still love them. It reinforces the impact of the discipline, too, and reminds you not to bear a grudge.

During the first series in the House, Lee, father to Jessica, was moved to tears as his little girl came up to him to say sorry for having a tantrum and for kicking him during the day. It was a real moment for Lee and their honesty with one another brought them much closer together.

Say 'No' as if you mean it

Julie needed to toughen up and learn to say 'no' to her strong-willed daughter. I wanted to teach her to push her voice out so that Ellie listened. A strong voice and a steady gaze get results.

- Speak from the diaphragm, not from the throat.
- Slow the pace of your voice, and make every word count.
- Use body language to convey the force of what you are saying and use your eyes to glare like they mean it. (I told Julie to imagine a man had put his hand on her bottom. 'Don't!' she declared and glared. Well, that worked!)
- If being assertive doesn't come naturally, then practise.

Dr Tanya says...
'Assertiveness is the ability to express problematic and difficult emotions in a way that is constructive.'

How to be assertive

In Chapter 1 (page 38) I talked about the importance of assertiveness as an integral part of self-esteem and self-belief in your parenting. Assertiveness is also a critical part of being able to reshape your child's behaviour effectively.

The keys to assertiveness are clarity (of voice and message), and confidence (in yourself and what you are doing). Phrase things simply and modulate your tone of voice and the way you articulate the words.

Several of the parents in the House found expressing their feelings quite difficult, and so being assertive was a problem for them. Remember that if your child is unable to tell whether you are angry, happy, amused or proud from your tone of voice, they will also find it hard to tell whether they are being praised or told off.

When you want your child to do something, try and detach your emotions from the situation and recognize that you are teaching them something important. One of the big challenges for a parent is to learn not to take personally the things their children say.

Assertiveness in children

If you start being assertive now, your children will learn from you how to be assertive. It is important that children learn to understand that experiencing negative feelings is a part of life. Aggression, tantrums, kicking and biting are all destructive behaviours that, if left unchecked, will isolate your child socially and cause you both anxiety. An assertive child will learn to say, 'I feel really cross with you mummy because...' rather than screaming, 'I hate you mummy! Go away!' while having a massive tantrum and rolling all over the floor. Assertiveness skills enable children to express themselves in a way that is constructive rather than destructive.

Facing up to anger

The first time your child moves you to anger can be a frightening experience, because the chances are you never expected to feel anything but love towards him or her. However, feeling angry does not mean a lack of love. People do shout at their kids occasionally – we are all human. Anger is a natural feeling and it is healthy to be able to express it in an appropriate, assertive and non-violent way. Appropriate behaviour in relation to children means non-physical, non-aggressive and calm.

Anger that is expressed and discussed can be understood and will eventually pass. However, not everyone is comfortable with expressing angry feelings and the danger is that unexpressed anger does not go away, it just goes deeper.

'One child having a tantrum is a nightmare, two... well I just feel out of my depth.'

(Tracey)

How do you cope when it gets too much?

- Find a place inside yourself to have a conversation with yourself and put some distance between you and the problem – it could be a peaceful image or a familiar song.
- Distract yourself by focusing on something else and disengaging from the noise.

Dr Tanya says...

'If you try to suppress anger repeatedly and over a long period of time, you run the risk eventually of exploding in response to a minor irritation in an uncontrollable and inappropriate manner which is out of all proportion with the event. The impact can be frightening – for you as well as your child – if it is directed at them.'

- Breathe: take deep breaths and consciously relax.
- Try to recognize that if you manage the problem in the short term, in the long term you won't have the problem.
- Keep things in perspective.
- Help yourself by recognizing that this is a normal developmental stage for your child – it is not a disaster. Your role is to help them through it and to learn from it.
- Don't get hung up on what others might be thinking (about the behaviour, the noise or your parenting techniques).
- Remember: if you start to shout and fill your child's head with negative thoughts, your words will reinforce the negative behaviour.
- Be self aware: know what your anger triggers are and plan to manage them.
- If you find yourself behaving very differently towards your child on some occasions than others – examine that behaviour and try to decide where it comes from.
- If necessary, remove yourself from the room until you have regained control. Don't wait until you've reached the point of no return.
- Look for support. If you're parenting with a partner, ask him or her to take over – and swap round.

All Paul wanted was for son Lewis to feel safe and happy. But Lewis's behaviour was causing both parents anxiety, and that anxiety was causing Paul to feel irritation and anger. Uncomfortable with his feelings, he was also fearful of 'losing it' with toddler Lewis when he had a tantrum. That fear may have been contributing unconsciously to keeping Lewis in his baby phase (see pages 86–7).

Anger is the 'fight' response to anxiety. Once Paul realized that, he was able to manage his feelings better. Paul and I spent time working on anger management techniques so that he got his anxiety into perspective and learned appropriate ways to ignore and contain Lewis's behaviour.

Many parents feel threatened as their babies begin to transform into toddlers. Compliant and cute baby behaviour tends to be replaced by moments of unpredictable rage and emotional outbursts such as, 'I hate you/ go away/ I don't want to...' etc, etc. For anyone with low self-esteem the apparently heartfelt cries can hit to the core. For someone unused to expressing anger, their inability to set effective boundaries and control their child can lead to an uncontrolled and inappropriate response.

Facing up to bad behaviour – yours

In Chapter 1 I talked a lot about the need for unified parenting and the fact that children pick up on parental mood and respond to it – usually in a negative way. (See page 37.)

This is just a reminder that children learn most of their behaviours from their parents and caregivers and from things that take place in the home. Schools and friends have their influence as children get older, but the foundation stones are set by you.

Many of the guidelines laid out here for children can apply equally to parents, too! If you find yourself arguing in an uncontrolled way in front of the children, be aware of the messages that you're giving your child – and give yourself a time out.

Dr Tanya says

'Arguing constantly in front of your children is damaging. One of the worst things for children is to grow up in a household full of hostility and conflict.'

And finally...

The good thing is that no matter how hard you find setting boundaries and being assertive with your child, they will appreciate it in the long run.

Making up and playing with your child is fun for both of you – and if you're all clear about what the house rules are, the positive outcome will bring you all even closer.

Dr Tanya's good behaviour programme

Take into account your child's age

- Babies do not realize they are separate beings from you.
- Until 3 years old your child's brain is not fully formed.
- Toddlers play up because they are trying to find their identity.
- If under 3 years old, show rather than tell a child what to do.
- At 3 years and over more explanation can be given.

Be a positive parent

- Be positive and nurturing towards your child.
- Take a unified approach to parenting.
- Follow the positive belief programme (see pages 42–3).
- Make time to play with your child (see page 48).

Follow three fundamental rules

- Reward good behaviour.
- Ignore bad behaviour.
- Be consistent.

Decide to take action

- Set clear behaviour boundaries.
- Put in place routines and structure.
- Stick to them.

Follow the programme

- Ask once nicely, ask once firmly.
- Explain the consequences. Mean them, and follow through.
- Make sure 'no' means 'no'.
- Use distraction techniques.
- Use role-play for learning.
- Encourage learning from others.
- Use time out.
- Explain why 'sorry' is necessary.
- Forgive with love and cuddles.
- Let it go.

Use time out

- as a first approach for entrenched behaviours.
- as a last resort for occasional naughtiness.
- as an immediate response to violent behaviour.
- as a period of cooling off if your child has lost control.

Reward good behaviour

- Create sticker charts for monitoring progress.
- Use treats as positive consequences.
- Reward positive outcomes.
- Be liberal with your praise, love and cuddles.
- Involve your child and play with them often.

Taming behaviour at other times

- At bedtimes, follow the peaceful sleep programme (see pages 78–9).
- At mealtimes, follow the friendly food programme (see pages 98–9).
- When away from home, follow the parenting on the move programme (see page 137).

Barbie

6

Parenting in Public

The central issue surrounding parental anxiety about their children's behaviour in public – especially when shopping, or during special occasions such as weddings, on outings or at Christmas – is the embarrassment of being judged by others. There is also the fear of possible danger if you lose control of your child.

The fear is understandable – especially if you don't feel in control of your child's behaviour. But the good news is that much of that fear can be faced head on and made to disappear. The first thing to say is: don't panic! As we have looked at in other chapters, children can pick up on your anxiety and if you're feeling out of control your child will feel out of control too.

The second thing to say is: Believe in yourself. All the guidelines outlined in the earlier chapters can be used in public – they just need adaptation to take into account that you are away from the home environment.

Your child is growing fast and has a brain that is responding like a sponge to everything that is going on around him or her. Time away from the home is full of interesting things which will stimulate your child's mind and interests – and help to develop individuality and life skills.

My wish is that once you have cracked the techniques outlined in this book you will look forward to and enjoy the times you have out with your child. There is nothing more enjoyable and delightful than a small person trying to make sense of the world in their unique way. The more you can be alongside them, enjoying and encouraging their view of the world, the closer your relationship will be.

Why do children play up in public?

There are many triggers for children, but at the root of many behaviours is a combination of excitement, anxiety and a sense that perhaps normal rules no longer apply. When you leave the familiar environment of home, the normal structure disappears. With no obvious boundaries and no familiar routine, children will test limits to find out where the new boundaries lie. You need to be prepared.

Plan ahead

- Tell your child where you're going and why, and also when you're coming back.
- Tell your child the kind of behaviour that you expect from them and explain that normal rules apply.
- Decide whether to use a sticker chart (see page 112), or another incentive to encourage good behaviour: *'If you are good, I will play on the computer with you for half an hour when we get home.'*
- Remember the fundamental rules:
Reward good behaviour.
Ignore bad behaviour.
Be consistent.
- If you are going to be gone for any period of time, take a toy or book with you that will comfort or distract your child.

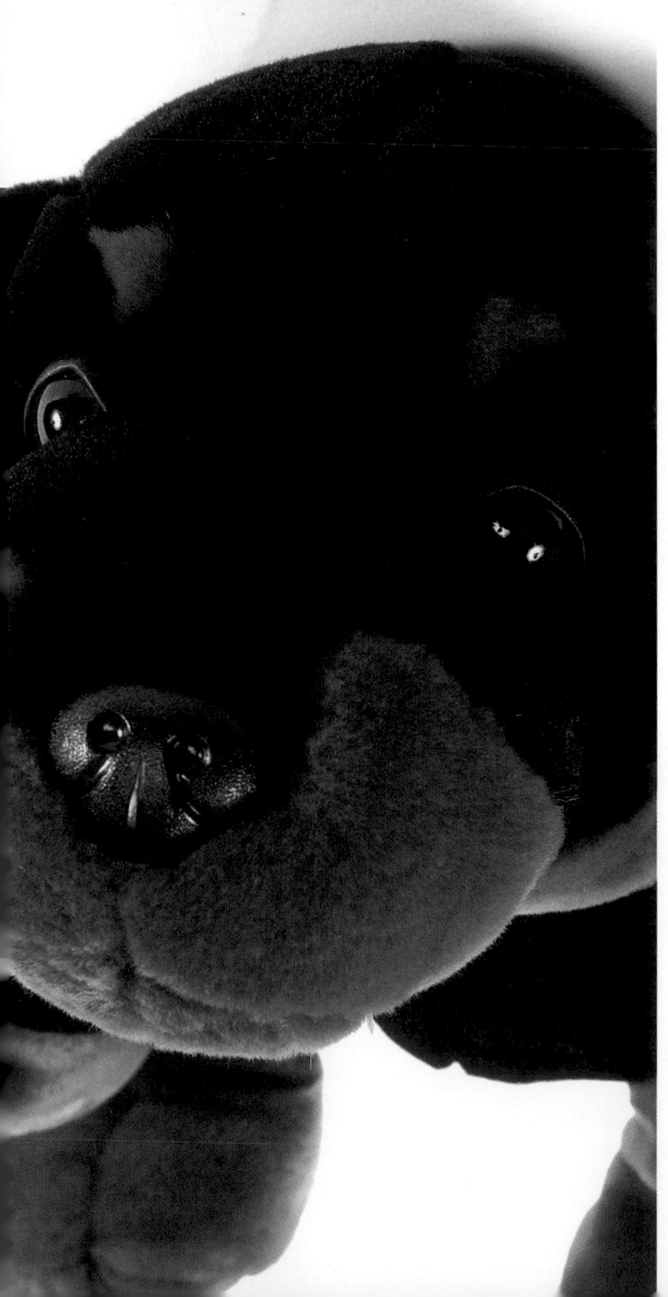

Understand what's going on

A child who plays up is not necessarily being deliberately naughty; there might be other factors at play.

Anxiety

If you are going somewhere new, or there are a lot of people around, your child may be overwhelmed or fearful of becoming separated from you. This is especially the case if you are having to rush and it is physically difficult for your child to keep up with you.

If they are old enough to understand, make sure you have explained where you are going, why you are going there and how you are going to travel. A child under three just needs to know that you are going out.

Take time to reassure and cuddle him or her. If you are in a public place or travelling, make sure they can see you at all times and hold their hand or make eye contact as much as possible.

Distraction techniques – such as playing with a favourite toy or drawing attention to colours, shapes and other interesting happenings – will also divert attention and put a space between their distress and the world around them.

Boredom

It is a well known fact that the shops that attract adults are much less appealing to children. That's life. But shopping has to get done, so here are some tips to keep the kids on your side:

- Depending on whether you are going to be in public or at someone else's house, take a favourite toy or game with you and some drawing paper and pencils.
- If you're food or clothes shopping, involve your children in the task and turn it into an exciting outing. (See Chapter 2: The Power of Play and Praise, for ideas.)
- If possible, plan how long you are going for and stick to that plan. Counting your child down to going home time will make it easier for both of you. ('After this shop there's only one more shop, and then we can go to the park.')
- Use warnings and incentives. Say:

'I'm going to ask you once nicely, and once firmly and if you don't stop we won't go into the toyshop on the way home.'
'On a count of 3: 1... 2... 3...'

'Can you stop whining now, please?'
'Will you stop that whining now.'
'Since you won't stop whining, we won't be going to the toyshop.'

- If an apology and pleading follows, stand firm, but give your child an incentive to prove themselves, such as behaving well for the next 15 minutes – and then you will review the situation.
- If the whining turns into a full-scale tantrum – use time out. See 'time out in public' on page 134.

Rage

A child in a rage may be out of control and possibly destructive. Getting what they want isn't necessarily going to calm them down. Their behaviour is often linked to disappointed expectations and an inability to take 'no' for an answer. He or she needs to be given time to 'cool off' and be given the tools to manage their moods and behaviour.

The only solution here is extreme ignoring – which means time out in public.

Attention-seeking

A child who simply wants your attention might embarrass or concern you with their noise level, but if you look closely you might see there is no genuine sign of distress or tears. If your child is used to getting your attention on demand, there is plenty of scope for playing up in public.

- Ignore the bad behaviour and use 'time out in public', if necessary.
- Use of an hourly sticker chart can work wonders if there is a promise of a treat at the end.

- Once they have calmed down, use distraction techniques to involve your child in what is going on.

Creating incentives

Children are naturally competitive – anyone who has experienced sibling rivalry in action or engaged in a battle of wills with a reluctant child will know only too well how strong-willed small people can be.

The competitive instinct is a healthy one and will help your child to survive in the big, wide world. The key to managing challenging behaviour is to help him or her to learn to channel their instincts, rather than to engage in a battle of wills. This is especially important when you are in public and a sudden rebellion could threaten the safety of your child or their brother or sister.

The competitive spirit loves being rewarded for achieving targets. Sticker charts, simple treats and rewards can be used to reinforce learning and will help your child to understand that there are clear guidelines to follow.

It is also helpful to encourage your child to notice the world around them. Try ploys such as:

- Who can see the first red bus?
- Who can see a squirrel up a tree?
- Who can put their gloves on before mummy does?

Incentives such as, pressing a button on the pelican crossing or to stop the bus, taking a ticket to board the bus, or to be next in line in the queue at the delicatessen counter can all help to keep your child's mind occupied and involved in what is going on around them.

If 'being on best behaviour' is the order of the day, feel no guilt at all about bribing your child with a treat. They need a major incentive to help keep themselves under control for an extended period of time.

Adapting techniques

Most of the approaches described in Chapter 2 and Chapter 5 can be used away from home, but there are two techniques that need some adaptation to work effectively: sticker charts and time out.

Sticker charts on the move

For a sticker chart to be effective away from home it needs to be quick and easy to use – and mobile.

The sticker chart principle can be turned into a mobile reward scheme in the shape of balls or other 'collectables', which are given to the child every few minutes as a reward for good behaviour, until they have gained enough to earn their treat.

Don't give your child an absolute target number of items. If you do, you will lose your flexibility to be able to treat them for less than the target, or keep them behaving well beyond that maximum.

A one-hour sticker chart

A simple one-task chart can be handy for a car journey, while sitting in a doctor's waiting room or if you simply want your child to control their tantrums or other unacceptable behaviour.

While in the House I asked Sarah to take her daughter Kelsey shopping. This was quite a challenge for Sarah because at home (see above), Kelsey had frequent tantrums and often threw herself on the ground.

Sarah went out armed with a mobile equivalent of a sticker chart in the form of a bag of coloured balls. For every 15 minutes that Kelsey was good, she would be given a coloured ball to put in her bag. Without being given an overall target, Kelsey was told that if she had a certain number of balls in the bag by the end of the day she would have a special treat.

The day wasn't without its problems, but overall Kelsey was awarded 8 out of 15 balls and mum Sarah decided that she deserved a treat for being so much better behaved than usual. It was a real breakthrough for both of them.

Lee and Louise used one to great effect while travelling in the car with Jessica and Hannah.

- Draw a rectangle on a sheet of paper and divide it into a grid: three rows of four squares. Each square represents 5 minutes of time.
- Every five minutes, give your child feedback on their behaviour. Good behaviour gets a sticker. Bad behaviour gets an unhappy face and requires an apology.
- If your child disregards your warnings, give them a second unhappy face within the 5-minute slot. This cannot be overturned with a sticker.
- If at the end of the hour there is only one box of two unhappy faces, it is fair to give your child their reward. After all, no-one is good all of the time.
- More than one box of two unhappy faces is a judgement call. You need to have the courage of your convictions and to follow through with the consequences you set if the sticker chart is to be effective.

'Tell your child before you leave home that normal behaviour rules apply.'

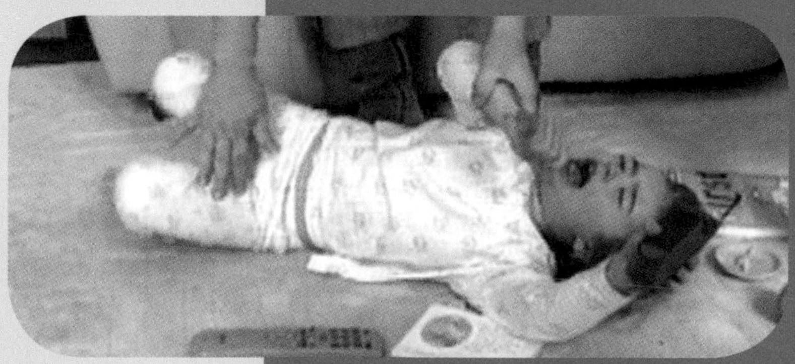

I asked Alyson and Richard to practise using the ignoring technique with daughter Lucie. They went out for the day to play crazy golf and were dreading Lucie's tantrums – especially during the car journey. With this technique they were able to contain Lucie's behaviour.

Once at the crazy-golf course they maintained their unified stance by walking together hand in hand ignoring Lucie's tantrums. Seeing that she was getting nowhere, she calmed down and joined them happily.

Time out in public

It isn't possible or appropriate to send your child away from you in public, and so a 'holding' version of time out is used.

- As with the home version of time out, tell you child when they are going into time out.
- Find somewhere to sit down, away from the crowds, and preferably facing something boring like a blank wall.
- Ignore your child's screams, shouts, cries or wishes to talk.
- Hold him or her firmly against your upper body, making sure you're holding them so that their head is well back (so they don't cause damage to you or themselves if they head-bang).
- Don't look at them, don't wipe their tears or have a chat or kiss them on the head, because that will give a mixed message that is completely wrong.
- Just sit them there, look away, and say absolutely nothing.
- Hold them firmly for 1 minute of each year of their age.
- When the allotted time is up, look your child in the eye and tell them briefly why they were in time out and that if the behaviour is repeated they will go back into time out again.
- If the tantrum is ongoing, again ask your child to stop: once nicely and once firmly.
- If they are unable to calm themselves down, explain that time out will be repeated if they don't stop.
- Repeat the process for the same period of time.
- Once your child has calmed down, explain why they were put into time out. Ask for an apology and give your child a cuddle.

Sarah used time out in public a lot with Kelsey to great effect – although I eventually had to talk to her about not over-using the technique. Time out needs to be balanced by lots of love and play – otherwise punishment starts to outweigh love and affection, which reinforces the negative behaviour.

- Then move on. Don't refer back to what happened during the day.
- At the first opportunity, reinforce the message by praising and cuddling your child for any good behaviour they exhibit.

If your child is still in a pushchair a variation on this version of time out can be used by containing them in their buggy and ignoring their behaviour. Again, do it for one minute of each year of their age.

Safety first

The biggest difference between being away from home and within your four walls is the potential for danger or threats to the safety of your child. For that reason it is important that you can count on your son or daughter to return to you when you call them. Count to three, with your child understanding that if they don't get to you by '3' there will be a consequence; e.g. being put in the buggy, hand being held firmly, or no treat.

Michelle perfected this technique with her sons Matthew and Ross while out in the park one day. Safety was a big concern for her because the two boys had a tendency to run off when they were out in public.

I taught her the principle of counting to three to retrain her boys' thinking and to reassure her that they would come when she calls. The technique got off to a fine start, but then it started to waiver.

Michelle reinforced the seriousness of what she was teaching them by using 'time out' in the buggy one at a time, to help them to understand what she was teaching them. Eventually the message got through and it gave Michelle an increased level of confidence in her parenting skills.

Initially, in order to turn the counting process into a game, it is useful to have some sweets or other incentives as treats to encourage your child to return to you.

- Explain to your child that if they run off you will count out loud and if they run back very fast they will earn a reward.
- If they don't come back straightaway then there will be a consequence.
- As with all the techniques, you need to be ready to follow through with the consequence if necessary.
- Say to your child: 'You are now staying here next to me until you have shown me that you know how to behave.'

Of course, if the danger is immediate and there is no time for niceties – shout loudly and assertively and run after the child who is in immediate danger.

Special pressures: special occasions

There are times in everyone's life when it's nice to let off steam, go crazy, and do the things you wouldn't normally do. This applies to children as well as adults. Children often choose to give in to this impulse when it is a special occasion of some sort and you are feeling vulnerable to the watchful eyes and criticism of others!

Unless your child is physically threatening another or causing wilful damage to your host's home in some way, keep your criticism of your child low-key and private. They have their pride too.

Make sure you have laid the ground rules before you set off on your journey, and when you arrive at your destination ask your child whether they remember what you said about behaviour.

Praise them for taking your instructions on board and, if appropriate, tell them that you know it will be difficult, but that you will be very proud of them if they behave, and that there will be a special treat when you get back home.

Be positive and encouraging of your child. Show them that you believe in their ability to be good and to do as you ask – and give them a hug.

'[Using these techniques] I was so relaxed and the situation was so relaxed. The boys were great.'

(Michelle)

Dr Tanya says...

'Believe in your child and believe in yourself as a parent. As any of the parents in the House of Tiny Tearaways will tell you, radical change is possible, and in many cases it's possible fast.'

Dr Tanya's parenting on the move programme

Face up to fear

- Believe in yourself.
- Believe in your child.

Plan ahead

- Tell your child:
  Where you're going.
  What to expect.
  What behaviour you expect from them.
- Take with you:
  A toy or a game to fend off boredom.
  A sticker chart or other incentive to keep them on track.

Be aware

- Be conscious of whether your child is:
  Anxious.
  Bored.
  Angry.
  Attention-seeking.

Use incentives

- Play I-spy games.
- Be competitive.
- Use distraction.
- Encourage fun and laughter.

Use behaviour-shaping techniques

- Create a mobile sticker chart.
- Use the counting technique.
- Follow the good behaviour programme (page 125).
- Use time out in public.

Remember the fundamental rules

- Reward good behaviour.
- Ignore bad behaviour.
- Stick to the programme.

Enjoy yourself

- Enjoy your child.
- Enjoy the occasion.
- Don't take the criticism of others to heart.
- Keep your sense of humour at all times!

Dr Tanya's Techniques for Taming Tearaways

When panic strikes and nothing seems to work, you need help fast! This section is for parents who need an 'at-a-glance' run down of each technique recommended in the book.

Dear Dr Tanya,

Where should I start?

Begin by laying the foundations, so your child understands what to expect:

- Set clear behaviour boundaries.
- Establish a regular daily routine.
- Don't cast your child in the role of monster.
- Introduce incentives, praise and rewards.
- Reserve time for playing with your child every day.
- Plan ahead.

What are the ground rules for success?

The same fundamental rules for successful behaviour-shaping are at the root of all the techniques:

- Reward good behaviour.
- Ignore bad behaviour.
- Be consistent.
- Follow through.

For general guidance see Chapters 1 and 2 for my *Positive Belief Programme* and my *Good Behaviour Programme.*

I need help in learning to play with my child

Stop thinking and start playing. Your child will soon show you what to do. Make time to play on a daily basis and you will start to create your own language, themes and ideas.

- Let your child lead.
- Actively comment on what your child is doing as they play.
- Comment on their progress.
- Reward their actions through praise and encouragement.
- Relax and have fun.
- Don't be afraid to be silly.
- Make everyday chores into opportunities for play.
- Make shopping a game.
- Allow kids to let off steam without over-control.
- Treat each child like an individual.
- Encourage role-play and dressing up.
- Be enthusiastic and smile!

For general guidance see Chapter 2 and my *Creative Play Programme.*

How do I create a sticker chart?

The main rules for a creating a sticker chart are:

- Decide on the time frame and the activities to be monitored.
- Create a grid and fill in names and actions.
- Involve your child in its creation.
- Decide on the treat and the consequences.
- Follow through consistently.

For step-by-step guidance see pages 112-13 and 132.

What shall I do? My child...

... won't eat solid foods

You should first ensure that your child does not have a food phobia. (See Chapter 4)

- Start with finger play.
- Introduce messy play.
- Serve small portions.
- Stay calm and be patient.

... is a fussy eater

Young children are naturally fussy and suspicious of anything new, so you will need patience to get success.

- Don't give control over

food choice to your child.

- Make food and mealtimes fun.
- Don't fuss.
- Introduce positive food associations.
- Avoid snacking between meals.

... won't sit at the table

This is a behavioural issue.

- Use 'Ask once nicely, once firmly'.

See 'Action' on page 142.

... won't use a knife and fork

Using implements takes practise. Make sure your child is comfortable with other forms of self-feeding first.

- Use yourself as a role model to show your child how to eat.
- Encourage other forms of self-feeding with a spoon or fingers.
- Eat with other children to encourage learning by association.
- Be patient and don't lose your cool.

For general guidance see Chapter 4 and my *Friendly Food Programme.*

Top Food Tips

- **Food phobias can take a long time to overcome.**
- **Children who are uncomfortable with wet foods are often anxious about mess.**
- **Messy eating is about learning.**
- **Allow children to move on from the bottle and the high chair.**
- **Don't use toys, books or TV to distract.**
- **Avoid showing anxiety around food.**
- **Reward success.**

... won't go to bed

You control your child's bed-times, not your child. Establish a routine and be firm.

- A regular bedtime routine is crucial to establish good sleep habits and sleep cues.
- Remember that sleep deprivation contributes to daytime behaviour problems.
- Use rapid return and gradual withdrawal techniques to encourage new behaviour-shaping.

... keeps getting out of bed

Your child has developed a behavioural habit that will need to be broken. It will take some persistence, but if you are consistent you should get effective results.

Rapid return

Purpose: To give your child the clear message that: *'Bedtime is not up for negotiation. You're safe. You have to stay in bed.'*

Sleep diary

Purpose: To measure lengths of time asleep as well as number of wakings. To enable you to see that progress is being made even when you have returned your child to bed dozens of times in one night.

... wakes in the night and comes into my bed

There are two parts to this problem (1)Your child has learnt inappropriate sleep cues and needs the comfort of you and your bed to settle back to sleep and (2) Your child needs to learn to sleep through the night in their own bed. You need to change the pattern.

Healthy sleep cues
Purpose: Healthy sleep cues remind your child that:
'It's time to go to bed, you are loved and safe, you will soon settle to sleep.'

Gradual withdrawal
Purpose: To give your child the reassurance that:
'I'm here. I'm not going to abandon you but I'm not going to play.'

... *won't sleep*

All children will sleep eventually if they are tired.

- Is it unusual behaviour? Make sure he or she is not unwell or upset about something.
- Have they been napping through the day? Consider cutting out the nap.
- Is it wilful behaviour? Use ignoring and rapid return.

For general guidance see Chapter 3 and my *Peaceful Sleep Programme.*

...*won't stop being naughty*

However the unwanted behaviour expresses itself (biting, hitting, throwing, swearing, tantrum, screaming etc) the approach to controlling and re-shaping it is the same.

Prevention

- Be a positive role model yourself.
- See trouble coming and distract your child.
- Up your level of praise, reduce the level of negative comments.
- Introduce incentives, praise and reward.

Action

- Respond to naughtiness fast and consistently.
- Give a warning.
- Ask once nicely, ask once firmly.
- Explain the consequences (and make them realistic)
- Make sure 'no' means 'no'.
- Totally ignore bad behaviour.
- Follow through

Use time out in extreme circumstances (see below).
Explain the consequences.
Ask for an apology.
Forgive and forget (let it go).
Use praise at the first next opportunity.

Top Sleep Tips

- **Children can settle themselves to sleep on their own from 6-12 months onwards.**
- **Sleep patterns sometimes get worse before they get better – but persevere.**
- **Involve your child in creating their bed and sleep area.**
- **Don't negotiate on bedtimes.**
- **Don't give in to the temptation of night-time snuggling with your child.**
- **Use incentives to encourage your child to settle to sleep.**
- **Children who suffer from night terrors are not necessarily in distress – don't be tempted to take them into your bed.**

Time out

Purpose: Time out is an extreme form of ignoring. It sends a message that: *'You are being excluded and ignored until you calm down and say sorry (and mean it).'*

See page 116-17 for the rules of time out

I've tried using Time Out but...

...it just doesn't work.

If it has never worked you need to review the way you are using it.

- Make sure that you ignore your child completely.
- Do not talk through the door.
- Put them in time out for exactly 1 minute for each year of their life (no more, no less).
- Ignore every behaviour, including kicking, screaming and sounds of destruction!
- Make sure it takes place in a location that is very boring, with no distractions.
- Your child must apologise sincerely at the end of the allotted period and understand why they were in time out.

... it's stopped working

You have been overusing the technique and it has lost its effectiveness. Use alternatives such as distraction and praising instead.

... the tantrums still won't stop

Your child hasn't yet learnt to manage his or her rage.

- Repeat time out until your child is calmer.
- Stick to the time out rules in each case.
- Make sure your child understands what they did wrong.

... I can't get him (or her) to listen to me

You are not gaining the respect of your child.

- Be more emphatic. Use your face and voice more expressively.
- Spend time focusing on improving assertiveness techniques.
- Be aware of your body language.
- Keep what you say simple and direct (don't try to reason or explain).

... I can't get him (or her) to stay in time out

This is linked to assertiveness (above) and is also related to persistence.

- If your child comes out of time out, return them immediately.
- Keep doing so until they get the message.
- This may take some time in the early stages.

... my child enjoys time out

Your child has turned a punishment into playtime.

- Time out should be no longer than one minute for each year of your child's life.
- Once the time is over your child comes out of time out – or has a warning and goes back in.
- If your child enjoys time out in their room, move the time out spot to a boring location.

For general guidance on behavioural techniques, see chapters 5 and 6, my *Good Behaviour* and *Parenting on the Move* programmes.

Dr Tanya's top tips for parenting

Be the adult

- Realise that your child needs a responsible parent, not a buddy.
- Be a positive role model for your child.

Plan ahead

- Develop a routine – and stick to it.
- Expect your child to play up when you are out – and take toys or games with you.

Keep calm

- Remember: a parent who is in control will be respected.
- Control your breathing by slowing it down and breathing through your diaphragm.
- Focus on relaxing your muscles: unfurrow your brow, relax your shoulders, unclench your fists or toes.
- Think about the non-verbal message you are giving out.
- If a child sees you are anxious they'll become anxious too.

Watch your attitude

- Be positive and constructive as often as possible.

Speak up

- Develop assertiveness skills.
- Project your voice with authority.
- Use body language to reinforce what you're saying.
- Manage your anger.
- Practise assertiveness skills.
- Remove yourself physically or mentally from sources of stress.
- Take time out if you're about to 'blow'.

Listen

- Don't talk at, listen to.
- Believe your child has something to say.
- Let your child lead on occasion.
- Be patient with their style of communication.
- Use drawing and play to find out what they are thinking.

Compromise

- Resolve contradictory parenting styles.
- Allow your child to negotiate sometimes.
- Don't expect perfection – or you'll always be disappointed.

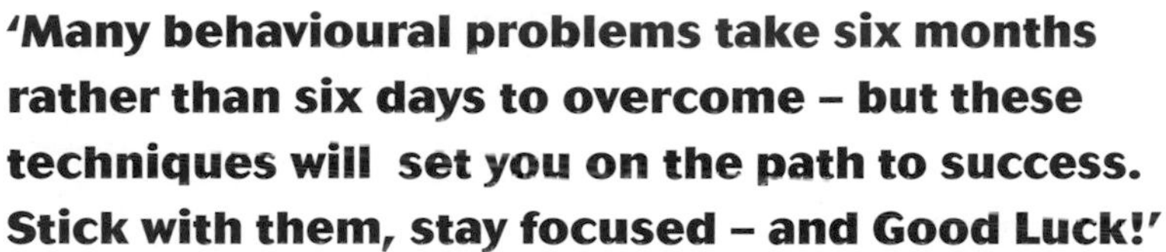

'Many behavioural problems take six months rather than six days to overcome – but these techniques will set you on the path to success. Stick with them, stay focused – and Good Luck!'

Keep off limits

- Don't argue in front of the children.
- Don't smack.
- Don't scream and shout.
- Be aware of the past.
- Understand that your past affects your parenting.
- Be aware of unresolved grief and unfinished business.
- Find ways of resolving past issues.
- If you are suffering hurt and pain, ask for help, if you need it.

Let go

- Let your child grow up.
- Allow them to make their own mistakes: remember that's how we learn.
- Recognise that life is not about keeping your child artificially happy.

Find a balance

- You are more than a parent, you are a person too.
- Try not to live your life through your child.

I'm worth it

- Make time for you too.
- Nurture self-esteem.
- Believe in your self.

Make couple time

- Plan time for yourselves alone.
- Talk about topics that do not involve work or the children.
- Take time to connect with each other.
- Make time and space for yourselves as a couple (without the children).

Your commitment

- Consider drawing up a parenting contract to reaffirm your expectations of your self, your co-parent and your child.

For more general guidance refer to Chapter 1 and my *Positive Belief Programme.*

police

8

A Life-Changing Formula

The thirteen families who came through the doors of the House of Tiny Tearaways during the four weeks of the first series were pioneers. They were courageous and – for the most part – they were desperate. They knew what they wanted to achieve but they had no idea whether it was possible. We were all in it together.

Every parent has the love and skill to transform their family using the techniques in this book. This chapter features recent updates from the families who participated in *The House of Tiny Tearaways*.

Writing this book has provided the perfect opportunity to get back in touch with the families who took part and to find out how life is now, nearly a year later. I wanted to know whether things had changed, whether they had had any problems, what had worked particularly well – and what they would recommend to other parents. Here they talk about their challenges, their successes and the lasting changes they've made at home.

I had no idea what to expect in response. Their feedback has been overwhelming and has reaffirmed to all of us involved that we have a dynamic and life-changing formula which transforms lives – permanently.

Week 1

Louise and Lee (Hannah and Jessica)

'Working with you has changed everything. We've moved house, the kids have changed schools and I'm working now as well. We'd never have been able to do that without your help. When I look back at footage from the first series I can't believe the situation we were in. Was that really us? It's all so different now.

Lee and I celebrated ten years as a couple recently and if we hadn't taken part in the programme we're not sure whether we'd still be together. It really helped our relationship. The experience was life-changing for us and it brought us back together as a family.

I feel sometimes as if I've walked out of my life and stepped into somebody else's. I used to sit and watch mums with their kids and I never felt I was part of a real family because I didn't have any confidence as a mother. Now, if I'm tempted to shout I remind myself, 'Who's the adult here and who's the child?' and just ignore their behaviour. I often praise the girls now just for being good. We have a calm bedtime routine, too, and we stick to it. It means Lee and I have time together.

We framed the contract that Hannah drew up with you and it's hanging in the family playroom. The girls refer to it a lot and it reminds us what we're meant to do.'

'Thank you, Tanya, from the bottom of our hearts. Our experience in the House changed everything... it brought us back together as a family.'

Paul and Nicky (Lewis)

'To sit down as a family and have a meal might seem the simplest thing in the world – but for us it's still amazing. We felt alone and isolated, and desperate to get Lewis's eating problem sorted out. You were a saviour to us, really. It was quite difficult to accept the fact that we were causing his problems, but you didn't make us feel bad – you made us think. It was a very emotional week and we had to face up to a lot of truths; but it was worth it.

The House was an artificial environment. At home you're on your own and real life can be tricky. I do sometimes think 'I don't have time to let him get messy'. It was tough at first and we still have odd days where Lewis won't want to know, but I'm proud of us because we've managed to stick to the things you told us to do. We no longer treat Lewis like a baby; we let him get messy when he's eating and we let him live his life. The change has been marvellous.

'To sit down as a family and have a meal might seem one of the simplest things in the world – but for us it's still amazing.'

Nicky and I both feel stronger now. The experience gave us a confidence boost and made us feel that, if we can tackle this, there are other things in life that we can tackle. It was a very, very positive experience.'

'Dr Tanya... keep doing what you're doing. A lot of people are listening... I want to tell you – you've got a big fan base in the 'hood!'

Nicola (Dante)

'Since working with you my family life has changed dramatically. I work full time, my confidence has sky rocketed and I'm not depressed anymore. Dante and I play together now and that's one thing I'm very, very happy about. We enjoy going shopping, too, and he doesn't throw tantrums. I listen to him more now and he talks very well. Since he's been home he has slept every night in his own bed. He loves his bed and he loves his room. I still use 'get up and pick up' when he gets up at night; but he generally just takes himself back to bed. We don't even exchange words.

After what Dante and me had gone through in the House, and what we had achieved, I was so pumped I couldn't wait to get home, because my mind was made up. I knew what I had to do. When I came home I wrote it all down and gave everyone copies. Both sides of the family agreed to stick to the rules. I am so happy and so proud. My whole family treats me differently now: they respect my decisions. Before, other people were controlling how I raised Dante because I wasn't confident in myself as a mother. Now, what I say is what I say.

You set the pace, Dr Tanya, and now I follow through daily. Routine, routine, routine: that's what works for me. And life is peachy!'

Week 2

Alyson and Richard (Lucie)

'Tanya, you made me realize that the things we do in later life are because of what's happened to us when we were younger. I would never have thought of the things that you came up with. I have been given my life back and I no longer worry all the time.

One thing in particular opened a million doors for me: you told me that every time Lucie cried it triggered a memory and made me feel the pain I felt when I was seven and my mum left us. I thought Lucie was feeling the same pain. You said, *'How can your daughter feel that pain, when you've never left her?'*

That one sentence changed my life. I was absolutely amazed – and I still am. At that moment I thought, 'What have I been doing? What have I been thinking?' I was giving in to Lucie but it wasn't doing her any good.

The second revelation was realizing that when Lucie was having her tantrums, there wasn't even a tear! I had thought she was upset and just wanted to comfort her. Being told, 'you don't need to worry' was the biggest thing to hear.

The experience has changed Richard's relationship with Lucie, too. We've still got some challenges, and I find it hard sometimes – but our lives are so much easier now.'

'It's not the children that need the help; it's the parents. We make them who they are.'

'I now have a strict routine with the boys and absolutely everything in my life has changed for the better.'

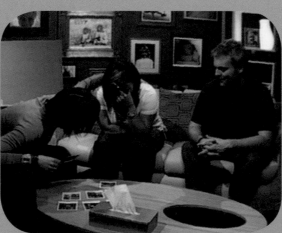

Michelle (Matthew and Ross)

'If I hadn't had the opportunity to work with you, I don't know what I would have done. Everything you can possibly think of has now changed. I used to be so exhausted and would have done anything for a good night's sleep. Now I have a strict routine with the boys and I have time for myself.

The idea of coming home was really scary. But I did exactly what we'd done in the House and stuck to the rules. From the first night the boys went to bed really well and, although the first couple of nights were a challenge, they soon understood that 'this was it'. The Supermum T-shirt I made on the last day in the House is a real symbol of what we had been through. It helped me to get past my low point.

My friends and family now know not to call between 6 and 8 o'clock in the evening because it's my time with the boys. We have a fixed routine of tea, play and bath. I had never had a routine before and it's made a real difference.

They are brilliant boys. They're just boisterous like any other children. They have even more energy – but they're more content and happier for it. I feel in control now and I've got more patience, too. I have an authority and a belief in myself.'

Paula and Steve (Jacob and Isaac)

'Mealtimes are so much easier these days: Jacob eats well all the time and Isaac has gone from strength to strength. I used to be so frightened to go out, but we can take them anywhere now. We have kept up the practice of going to restaurants. Seeing them tucking in means everything, and we are no longer anxious. At weekends we eat together, but during the week we step back. If Isaac doesn't eat we go back to using stickers as an incentive.

I went backwards during our first week home. I was on my own and was convinced I wasn't doing things right. You helped me to understand that it's about being relaxed and making food fun rather than a big issue – so we kept up the family picnics too. They really helped Isaac to progress and even if he only eats half his food these days I don't worry.

It was such an emotional week for us. We have learned not to show anxiety or be uptight at mealtimes and socialization helps a lot. Kids learn from each other and mealtimes are more of a social occasion now. There are often lots of people around the table and lots of talking – so there's no pressure.'

'Mealtimes are much more of a normal social occasion now... there's no pressure .'

Week 3

Sara and Darren (Harrison)

'Being in the House gave us a different perspective and you made us realize that we needed to change our parenting style. We now understand that focusing on the good is more effective than shouting; and that the quality of time and how you spend it with your child is very important. We now play and read with Harrison for 40 minutes to an hour every day, and at weekends his dad takes him to work to get messy and 'do mixing'. He's happy now and not as anxious. Getting him to school used to be a nightmare, but now he goes, 'Love you. Bye!'

The change helped us to take the decision to move to Australia – we could never have considered it before. And we're expecting a new baby, too. Harrison is much more loving these days and is really looking forward to it.

We have had no problems since we got back home and no relapses. He actually asks to go to bed now! He doesn't kick or punch any more either. We use sticker charts a lot and going riding is his big reward. I focus on keeping calm when Harry is naughty, so he listens to me more. He still eats a lot of bread and butter, but he eats bananas now, too, and likes chicken and gravy. He's not too bad at getting dirty either.'

'The quality of time and how you spend time with your child is very important.'

Sarah (Kelsey)

'Tanya, I needed someone to point me in the right direction and that's just what you did. Kelsey and I are a lot closer now and I understand her much better. We do still argue sometimes – but it's not as frequent now and it's a much better quality relationship all together. These days we're mum and daughter, and we are much closer. We play a lot more now, too; I hardly ever need to use time out and never need to restrain her. If necessary I send her to cool off in her bedroom, but usually she stops playing up after a word or two from me.

We still have our moments – and it's an ongoing process – but because my attitude towards Kelsey has changed, she has changed too. It was very important for me to have made up with my dad. He backs me up now; we have a much stronger relationship and I am happy for him to be the lenient granddad.

You were absolutely brilliant. From day two you said you knew what the problem was and how to solve it – and you were right! You just hit the nail on the head with everything. I'm glad I came to the House; I'd do it again if I needed to because it's changed the way we work.'

'Kelsey never comes home screaming any more. Now she cries if she wants me to stay instead.'

Dr Tanya says...
'Ryan's behaviour was environment-specific and he played up only when in his home. For that reason I suggested that they left the House on day two and I worked with them over the phone and treated them when they were at home.'

Fiona and Mark (James and Ryan)

'There have been immeasurable differences in our family since we worked with you, and life is now much calmer. Although on the surface our circumstances weren't as extreme as some of the other families, for us life had become a nightmare because of Ryan's behaviour. He was throwing things the whole time – it didn't matter whether he was happy or not. You don't have to be in an extreme situation to feel you have a big problem.

Our concern was that if Ryan didn't learn to control his anger now, it would be much more difficult when he got older. Our confidence had taken a real knock and we didn't know what to do. We had been using time out, but we hadn't done it consistently. Once we began using your approach to the letter, Ryan's throwing stopped almost immediately.

It was brilliant to have you looking over our shoulders and telling us what to do.

Although Ryan still has trouble dealing with 'No', I can take him out now and he'll be happy. He's still a real livewire and knows his own mind, but we are using distraction and incentives rather more than time out now.

It was so good to hear someone say, 'you're nearly right – you just need to do this.' We're really grateful; your advice was invaluable.'

'You don't have to be in an extreme situation to feel you have a big problem.'

'I've definitely got more confidence as a parent now.'

Week 4

Anita (Jaden)

'I used to try lots of different discipline techniques with Jaden, but I was a bit wishy washy in my approach. Now I know that what he needs is a consistent combination of discipline and positive praise.

Some weeks can still be a nightmare, but the most important lesson for me was learning to keep calm: the calmer I am, the better Jaden behaves. Every now and then he will say a naughty word – but he's not swearing at me, he does it because he's frustrated with himself. If I use the distraction technique it works wonders. I engage with him much more now and don't get embarrassed in public either. I use positive praise a lot and have plenty of one-on-one time with him.

I had no adjustment problems when we got home because you had showed me what to do – within a week of coming home I was able to walk around town without worrying. On the bad days I would use time out, but now I keep it only for swearing and hitting. Distraction and praising are the techniques I use most often. I've definitely got more confidence as a parent now.'

Tracey and Bulent (Hakan, Konur and Emir)

'Family life has improved a lot; now we take the boys out more and have much more confidence. Our time in the House was a real wake-up call. Bulent and I asked ourselves what sort of example we were setting with our communication, and we don't argue in front of the boys any more.

The twins are doing really well, we don't dress them the same any more and we treat them as individuals. Soon after the programme I took them out of nappies. The staff at the early years centre have said that they have seen a big change in them and they are starting to shine.

Part of the twins' behaviour problems is due to their speech problem, so it will take time to get right. But I am sure they will get there. Hakan is still our little superstar and with the twins in bed by 6.30pm, Haken gets $1\frac{1}{2}$ hours on his own to spend with us. He is such a good boy and we are so proud of him. Children are an amazing gift and they're not small for long. It's important to enjoy them.

We want to thank you for all your help. we will never forget the time spent with you. You touched our lives in a special way – thank you.'

'Our time in the House was a real wake-up call. What sort of example were we setting?'

'Alan and I have got more time together now and bedtimes aren't a nightmare any more.'

Alan and Julie (Ellie)

'Life changed a lot for us when we left the house and the behaviour techniques are automatic for us now. We were lucky because the main changes happened almost immediately. By the second night I could settle Ellie to sleep after 15 minutes – and now she sleeps through the night. We keep to a strict bedtime routine now – even when we are on holiday. Sometimes, if she's had an exhausting day, we put her to bed as early as 5.30 or 6pm. Alan and I have got more time together and bedtimes aren't a nightmare any more.

Ellie still does have tantrums, but she's in her terrible twos. She is very bright and always wants to do new things. It's a challenge because she says she really loves time out and being in her room! She's still strong-willed and is growing up fast.

Being in the House was a really good experience and we're still in touch with the other families, which is brilliant.'

It is impossible to be a parent without your world changing forever. Parenting is both a joy and a challenge, but when problems emerge that are hard to resolve, the initial delight can turn into a nightmare. The parents who joined me in the House showed just how possible it is to turn around even the most extreme behavioural problem with a consistent, loving and firm approach.

The community aspect of the House was also important and many of the families are still in touch with each other. Having a support network makes a huge difference to a parent's ability to cope when the going gets tough. Friendships that you and your child make while they are toddlers often become important friendships for life.

If you love and praise your child, gain their respect and learn to manage behaviour consistently when they are young, you have laid solid foundations to help them find their way in life.

Dr Tanya says...
'Today's toddler is tomorrow's teenager. Bear that in mind when you're tempted to return to your old ways!'

Further Resources

Psychology, counselling and psychotherapy

Association of Child Psychotherapists
Holds a directory of accredited child psychotherapists; provides details of local child psychotherapists.
Tel: 020 8458 1690
Web: www.acp.uk.net

British Association for Counselling and Psychotherapy
Details of local counsellors and psychotherapists across the UK.
Tel: 0870 4435 252
Web: www.counselling.co.uk

British Psychological Society
Holds national register of chartered psychologists.
Tel: 0116 254 9568
Web: www.bps.org.uk

Traumatic Stress Clinic
Offers a specialist approach to the psychological assessment and treatment of children and their families following a trauma.
Tel: 020 7530 3666
Web: www.traumatic-stress.com/tsc

United Kingdom Council for Psychotherapy (UKCP)
National register of psychotherapists and can give details of local counsellors and psychotherapist.
Tel: 0870 167 2131
Web: www.psychotherapy.org.uk

Pregnancy & birth

ARC (Antenatal Results and Choices)
A charity providing non-directive support and information to parents during the antenatal testing process.
Tel: 0207 631 0285
Web: www.arc-uk.org

BirthChoiceUK
Information on birth options and where to have your baby.
Web: www.birthchoiceuk.com

Bliss
Premature baby charity offering a parental support and advice network for families whose babies need special or intensive care.
Tel: 0500 618140
Web: www.bliss.org.uk

fpa (formerly Family Planning Association)
Provides confidential advice on sexual health, contraception, emergency contraception and pregnancy options.
Tel: 0845 310 1334
Web: www.fpa.org.uk

Maternity Alliance
Campaigning, research, training and information on maternity services and rights.
Tel: 020 7490 7638
Web: www.maternityalliance.org.uk

National Childbirth Trust
Information on pregnancy and babycare, antenatal classes, local groups and nearly new sales.
Tel: 0870 444 8707
Web: www.nctpregnancyandbabycare.com

Tommy's
Advice to improve the chance of a healthy pregnancy. Information line plus a range of free publications.
Tel: 0870 777 30 60
Web: www.tommys.org

Twins and Multiple Birth Association (TAMBA)
Charity providing information and mutual support networks for families of twins, triplets and more.
Tel: 0870 770 3305
Web: www.tamba.org.uk

Breastfeeding

The Department of Health's recommendations are that breast milk is the best form of nutrition for infants. Exclusive breastfeeding is recommended for the first 6 months of a baby's life, and beyond.

Association of Breastfeeding Mothers
Run voluntarily by mothers. There is a 24-hour helpline to a qualified breastfeeding counsellor and list of regional support groups.
Tel: 020 7813 1481
Web: www.abm.me.uk

Breastfeeding Network
Information about breastfeeding (as well as medical articles) and a popular FAQ section.
Tel: 0870 900 8787
Web: www.breastfeedingnetwork.org.uk

La Leche League (GB)
Promotes breastfeeding and offers a support helpline.
Tel: 0845 120 2918
Web: www.laleche.org.uk

Parenting

Dads UK
Dads UK is the first and only helpline for single fathers.
Helpline: 07092 391489
Web: www.dads-uk.co.uk

Families Need Fathers
Tel: 020 7613 5060
Helpline: 0870 760 7496
Web: www.fnf.org.uk

Fathers Direct
For all dads, from fathers-to-be to more experienced dads.
Web: www.fathersdirect.com

Gingerbread
Self-help organization for lone-parent families.
Tel: 0800 018 4318
Web: www.gingerbread.org.uk

Grandparents' Association
Provides an advice line for information on all aspects of grandparenting.
Tel: 01279 444 964
Web: www.grandparents-federation.org.uk

Home-Start
Provides support to parents of under-fives and recruits parents as volunteers to offer friendship and support to other parents.
Tel: 0800 068 6368
Web: www.home-start.org.uk

Meet-a-Mum Association (MAMA)
Provides friendship and support to mothers and mothers-to-be.
Helpline: 020 8768 0123
Web: www.mama.org.uk

National Association of Citizens Advice Bureaux
Free advice on issues including pregnancy.
Tel: Local numbers only
Web: www.citizensadvice.org.uk

National Council for One Parent Families
Runs an information service, campaigns and lobbies to change the law and improve provisions for lone parent families.
Tel: 020 7428 5400
Helpline: 0800 018 5026
Web: www.oneparentfamilies.org.uk

One Parent Families Scotland
Tel: 0800 018 5026
Web: www.opfs.org.uk

Parentline Plus
Operates a national freephone telephone helpline for parents and carers of children in stressful and other situations.
Helpline 0808 800 2222
Web: www.parentlineplus.org.uk

Childcare

4Children
The national organization for out-of-school care, with information on afterschool clubs and out-of-school care in England, Wales and Scotland.
Tel: 020 7512 2100
Web: www.4children.org.uk

Childcare Link
Government information about national and local childcare.
Freephone 08000 96 02 96
Web: www.childcarelink.gov.uk

Daycare Trust
The national childcare campaign: promotes affordable childcare, provides information to parents, employers, policy-makers and providers.
Tel: 020 7840 3350
Web: www.daycaretrust.org.uk

National Childminding Association of England and Wales
Promotes quality, registered childminding.
Tel: 0800 169 4486
Web: www.ncma.org.uk

National Council of Voluntary Child Care Organisations (NCVCCO).
NCVCCO is the umbrella organization for voluntary childcare organizations in England.
Tel: 020 7833 3319
Web: www.ncvcco.org

Children

www.britkid.org
Focuses on the issues of race and racism and is aimed at schools. Includes useful web links.

Bullying Online
This online organization provides information and advice for parents and their children. They run an email advice service.
Email: help@bullying.co.uk
Web: www.bullying.co.uk

Childline
Provides a free 24-hour helpline and support for children and young people.
Tel: 0800 1111
Web: www.childline.org.uk

It's not your fault
NCH website offering information and support to children and teenagers whose parents are divorcing or separating.
Tel: 0845 7626579
Web: www.itsnotyourfault.org

Kidscape
Kidscape is the registered charity committed to keeping children safe from bullying, harm or abuse.
Tel: 020 7730 3300
Helpline: 08451 205 204
Web: www.kidscape.org.uk

Healthcare

Association for Post Natal Illness
Support for mothers.
Tel: 020 7386 0868
Web. www.apni.org

Community Practitioners' and Health Visitors' Association
UK professional body representing registered nurses and health visitors.
Tel: 020 7939 7000
Web: www.msfcphva.org

Cry-sis
Helpline for parents with crying and sleepless children.
Tel: 020 7404 5011
Web: www.cry-sis.com

Foundation for the Study of Infant Deaths
Leading cot death charity working to prevent cot death and promote baby health to parents, carers and professionals.
Tel: 0870 787 0554
Web: www.sids.org.uk

SureStart
Aims to improve the health and wellbeing of families and children.
Tel: 0870 000 2288
Web: www.surestart.gov.uk

Institute of Child Health
British research into the study and treatment of childhood disease.
Web: www.ich.ucl.ac.uk

NHS Direct
National helpline offering medical guidance and health information.
Tel: 0845 4647
Web: www.nhsdirect.org.uk

Special needs

Contact a Family
Charity offering support to parents of children with special needs and disabilities.
Tel: 0808 808 3555
Text: 0808 808 3556
Web: www.cafamily.org.uk

Council for Disabled Children
Information for parents and details of organizations offering services and support for disabilities and special educational needs.
Tel: 020 7843 1900
Web: www.ncb.org.uk

Disabled Parents Network
National organization of and for disabled people who are parents or who hope to become parents.
Tel: 0870 241 0450
Text: 0800 018 9949
Web: www.disabledparentsnetwork.org.uk

Gifted Children's Information Centre
Assessment of gifted, dyslexic, left-handed children or adults, or those with Asperger's syndrome or ADHD. Offers counselling, and advice for parents and help with negotiating with schools and local authorities.
Tel: 0121 705 4547

Talking Point
A website about speech and language development that provides quality information and signposts people to organizations that can help further.
Tel: 020 7674 2799
Web: www.talkingpoint.org.uk

Bereavement

Cruse Bereavement Care
Help for bereaved people of any age through counselling, advice, publications and mutual support. It has 160 local branches.
Tel: 0870 167 1677
Web: www.crusebereavementcare.org.uk

The Child Bereavement Trust
Charity with resources for families who've lost a baby or child, and for children who've suffered the death of a sibling or parent.
Tel: 01494 446648
Web: www.childbereavement.org.uk

The Compassionate Friends
A self-help organization set up by and for bereaved parents.
Tel: 0845 123 2304
Web: www.tcf.org.uk

The Miscarriage Association
Support for those who have suffered the loss of a baby during pregnancy.
Tel: 01924 200799
Scotland: 0131 334 8883
Web: www.miscarriageassociation.org.uk

SANDS (Stillbirth and Neonatal Death Society)
A national self-help organization that provides support for parents whose baby died at or soon after birth.
Tel: 020 7436 5881
Web: www.uk-sands.org

Mental health

Mencap National Centre
Services, advice and support for people with learning difficulties, their families and carers.
Tel: 0808 808 1111
Web: www.mencap.org.uk

MIND
Network of local centres, working for a better life for everyone with experience of mental distress in England and Wales.
Tel: 020 8215 2242
Web: www.mind.org.uk

SANE
Practical information, emotional support and crisis care for people affected by mental health problems.
Tel: 020 7375 1002
Helpline: 0845 767 8000
Web: www.sane.org.uk

Samaritans
Provides 24-hour confidential emotional support for those experiencing feelings of distress or despair.
Tel: 0845 790 9090 (UK)
Tel: 1850 609090 (RoI)
Web: www.samaritans.org.uk

Young Minds
A national charity concerned with the mental health of children and young people.
Tel: 0800 018 2138
Web: www.youngminds.org.uk

Relationships

Relate
National charity providing couple counselling for those with relationship problems.
Tel: 01788 573241
0870 6012121 (Counselling service)
Helpline: 0845 130 4010.
Web: www.relate.org.uk

BBC websites

www.bbc.co.uk/bbcthree/tv/tiny_tearaways
www.bbc.co.uk/health
www.bbc.co.uk/parenting
The BBC websites includes a comprehensive advice and information as well as links to a wide range of resources.

Also available:
Little Angels by Dr Tanya Byron and Sasha Baveystock, (BBC Books, 2003)

Acknowledgements

With love and thanks to:
My amazing husband Bruce and my darling children Lily and Jack (who kept my heart and soul together) to my best friend and business partner Sam Richards (who kept my spirit together) and to the consultant clinical psychologist Jo Douglas (who kept my head together). And to all the Tiny Tearaways team, especially: Kidge, Claudia, Toby, Sherpa, Laura and Martin.

The House of Tiny Tearaways Team (series one):
Executive Producers: Laura Mansfield, Martin Scott; **Executive Editor:** Steve Kidgell; **Series Producer:** Iain Hollands; **Series Director:** Kate Douglas Walker; **Designer:** James Dillon; **Titles Music:** Blair MacKichan; **Senior Producers:** Toby Gorman, Anna Meadows, Katie McAfee, Tom Edwards, James McKinlay; **Producers:** Maggie Kelleher, Megan Ellis, Simone O'Neill, Alex Cross, Sophie Lloyd, Sean Hancock, Peter Brown, Tom McDonald, Ros Malthouse, Lucy Croft, Ashley Gorman, Dan Clapton, Meriel Beale; **Production Executive:** Claire Bridgland; **Unit Manager:** Karen Barton; **Production Managers:** Nick Badham, Letty Kavanagh, Jo Alloway; **Directors:** Vaughan Dagnell, Jo Siddiqui, Ken Smith, Carrie Horne, Shelley Kingston, Leigh McSwann, Ollie Bartlett, Clare Slessor, Alona Ochert, Richard Watsham, James Bainbridge; **Assistant Producers:** Vickie Ager, Edward Tuke, Stephen Lovelock, Heather McGeever, Richard Wakefield, Chloe Huntly, Amy Robbins; **Researchers:** Alex Scott, Sarah Ladbury, Stephen Pain, Cat Hoskin, Sarah Udal; **Art Department:** Dick Lunn, Tayyaba Irhzaali, Mel Stenhouse, Laurie Law; **Production Team:** Kelly Ann McHale, Chris Logan, Alison Whitlock, Jenna Durdle, Lizzie Beasley, Lynne Greenshields, Donna Shawa, Natalie Jupp, Michelle Bacon, Noella Bible, Rachel Littlejohn, Beatrice Smith, Charlotte Linzell, Roberto Davoli, Oliver Barratt, David Cantor, Michelle McKeown, Amy Fernando, Roxanne Collins, Nick Dennis, Lee Reading, Elliot Carr-Barnsley, Harriette Allen, Yvonne Dickson, James Matthews, Ish Kalia, Sheena Abdulali, Nick Mack, Gea Broughton, Matt Edwards, Rachel Egenes, Kerry Hunt, Kevin Kilbey; **Sound:** Pete Vasey, John Pearce, Oliver France, Max Mills, Rufus Hine, Iain Ross, Steve Picco, Rick Simon, Dave Morton; **Post Production:** David Klafkowski, Jack Edney, Richard Swindells, Martin Begley, Riaz Bordie, John Smith, Charlie Phebey, Jack Hobbs, Dave Milkins, Phil Lepherd, Chris Joss, Cliff Homow, Dave Atkinson, Lennaart van Oldenborgh, Graham Taylor, Jason Reid, Leon Stuparich, Joe Pedder, Craig Langman, Dan Raymond, Steve Ralston, Tom Hemmings, Jamie Marsh, Dave McGurk, Jamie Riordan, Darren Leathley, Paul Crosby, Pete Saunders; **Cameras:** Charlie Bryan, Gary Beckerman, Phil Ingaells, Lucke Clayden, Barry McGuire, Craig Butchard, James Todd, Tom Parr, Alistair Miller, Russell Tate, Danny Sheldon, Carlo Tamburello, Bill Ashworth, Dibley, Jim Morris, Eddie Knight, Graham Stone, Evan Pugh, Kevin Mason, James Benfield, Oliver Anderson; **Engineers:** Dave Field, Steve Bartlett, Paul Nancollas, Daunton Todd, John Blake, Richard Pullen; **Lighting:** Nick Collier, Gary Wilis, Bob King, Dave Clayton, Peter Ward, Ryan Brazier, Malcolm Bray, Adrian Portimari; **Health & Safety:** Lisa Masterman; **Publicity:** Clare Gould

With special thanks to:
Stuart Murphy, Damien Kavanagh, Katherine Parsons, Suzanne Gilfillan and all the team at BBC 3; Helen Veale and the team at Outline Productions; Wayne Garvie, Richard Hopkins and the team at BBC Entertainment; Emma Shackleton at BBC Worldwide; Sarah Sutton; Annette Peppis; Rachel Barke, Rosie Gray, Fiona McGarrity, Matthew Frank and the team at RDF Rights; Barrie Woolston and all the team at Inmedia; Dr Alastair Sutcliffe, Floella Benjamin OBE, David King Taylor, Dr Mandy Byram, Judith Lask; The Farm; Roll to Record; Film and Television Services; Full Broadside Ltd; Anthony Smith Partnership; Up The Resolution - and most of all to all the families who took part in the first series and gave of themselves so generously. It was an honour and a pleasure to work with you.

BBC Worldwide would like to thank:
Jade Arklie, Tayla Watson Braithwaite, Milan Cato, Rebecca Dennis, Robyn Gray, Douglas Grobvic, Tyler Hayles, Mya O'Connor, Alexander Pleasants, Jake Wallenda, and James.

Picture credits

Index